Pathfinder® Guides

Acknowledgements

My thanks for the valuable advice and numerous useful leaflets that I obtained from the local authorities and the various tourist information centres throughout the area.

Text:	Neil Coates
Photography:	Neil Coates
Editor:	Ark Creative UK Ltd
Designer:	Ark Creative UK Ltd

This product includes mapping data licensed from Ordnance Survey® with the permission of the Controller of Her Majesty's Stationery Office. © Crown Copyright 2010. All rights reserved. Licence number 150002047. Ordnance Survey, the OS symbol and Pathfinder are registered trademarks and Explorer, Landranger and Outdoor Leisure are trademarks of the Ordnance Survey, the national mapping agency of Great Britain.

ISBN: 978-1-85458-505-9

While every care has been taken to ensure the accuracy of the route directions, the publishers cannot accept responsibility for errors or omissions, or for changes in details given. The countryside is not static: hedges and fences can be removed, field boundaries can alter, footpaths can be rerouted and changes in ownership can result in the closure or diversion of some concessionary paths. Also, paths that are easy and pleasant for walking in fine conditions may become slippery, muddy and difficult in wet weather, while stepping stones across rivers and streams may become impassable.

If you find an inaccuracy in either the text or maps, please write to Crimson Publishing at the address below.

Printed in Singapore. 1/10

First published in Great Britain 2010 by Crimson Publishing, a division of:
Crimson Business Ltd,
Westminster House, Kew Road, Richmond, Surrey, TW9 2ND

www.totalwalking.co.uk

A catalogue record for this book is available from the British library.

Front cover: Packhorse bridge and village centre at Wycoller
Previous page: Rombalds Moor viewed from The Buck Stones outcrop

Contents

Approximate walk times

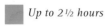 *Up to 2½ hours*   *3–4 hours* 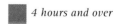 *4 hours and over*

*The walk times are provided as a guide only and are calculated using an
average walking speed of 2½mph (4km/h), adding one minute for each 10m
(33ft) of ascent, and then rounding the result to the nearest half hour.*

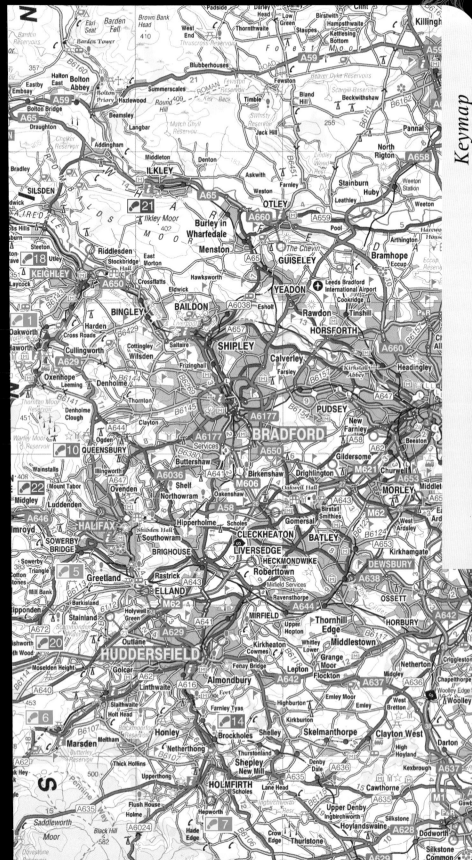

Walk	Page	Start	Nat. Grid Reference	Distance	Time	Height Gain
Blackstone Edge & Reservoirs	16	The White House Inn	SD 967178	5 ½ miles (8.9km)	2 ½ hrs	390ft (120m)
Cheesden Valley	29	Ashworth Moor Reservoir	SD 829160	6 ½ miles (10.5km)	3 hrs	770ft (235m)
Cliviger Gorge	78	Holme Chapel	SD 879279	6 miles (9.7km)	4 hrs	1,750ft (535m)
Cononley, Lothersdale & Holme Beck Valley	85	Cononley	SD 990468	8 miles (13km)	4 ½ hrs	1,505ft (460m)
Cowpe Moss & The Famine Road	71	Cowpe, Rawtenstall	SD 834214	7 ½ miles (12km)	4 hrs	1,210ft (370m)
Crimsworth Dean, Walshaw & Hebden Dale	75	Midgehole, Hebden Bridge	SD 988292	8 ¼ miles (13.3km)	4 hrs	1,310ft (400m)
Delph, Castleshaw & Harrop Edge	53	Wool Road, Uppermill	SD 995065	7 miles (11.3km)	3 ½ hrs	1,095ft (335m)
Haworth & The Worth Valley	12	Haworth church	SE 029372	3 ½ miles (5.6km)	2 hrs	490ft (150m)
Healey Dell	34	Broadley Old Station	SD 879164	5 ½ miles (8.9km)	3 hrs	885ft (270m)
Heber's Ghyll & Rombalds Moor	65	Ilkley	SE 100473	8 ½ miles (13.7km)	4 hrs	1,115ft (340m)
Heptonstall & Colden Clough	37	Heptonstall	SD 986280	5 ½ miles (8.9km)	3 hrs	1,145ft (350m)
Hepworth's Hidden Gem	24	Hepworth	SE 163067	4 ½ miles (7.2km)	2 ½ hrs	800ft (245m)
Ickornshaw & Earl Crag	18	Ickornshaw church	SD 967430	4 ¼ miles (6.8km)	2 ½ hrs	850ft (260m)
Langfield Common, Stoodley Pike & Cragg Vale	81	Walsden Station	SD 931222	10 miles (16km)	4 ½ hrs	1,115ft (340m)
Luddenden Dean, Midgley Moor & Churn Milk Joan	68	Jerusalem Farm, Luddenden Dean	SE 036278	8 ½ miles (13.7km)	4 hrs	1,065ft (325m)
Mankinholes & The Rochdale Canal	14	Lobb Mill Picnic Site, Todmorden	SD 955246	4 miles (6.4km)	2 hrs	590ft (180m)
Marsden Moor & March Haigh Reservoir	22	The Green, Marsden	SE 047116	4 ¾ miles (7.6km)	2 ½ hrs	1,000ft (305m)
Norland Moor	20	Norland Moor	SE 055218	4 ¾ miles (7.6km)	2 ½ hrs	785ft (240m)
Ogden Reservoir, Nab Hill & Ovenden Moor	32	Ogden Reservoir, north of Halifax	SE 065309	6 miles (9.7km)	3 hrs	620ft (190m)
Piethorne Valley	47	Ogden Reservoir, Newhey	SD 952122	5 ½ miles (8.9km)	3 hrs	1,245ft (380m)
Ponden Kirk, Alcomden Stones & the Brontë Moors	50	Stanbury	SE 012371	6 miles (9.7km)	3 ½ hrs	1,000ft (305m)
Ripponden & The Ryburn Valley	62	Booth Wood Reservoir	SE 031165	6 ¼ miles (10km)	3 ½ hrs	1,280ft (390m)
Steeton Moor & Newsholme Dean	56	Keighley (Redcar) Tarn	SE 038422	7 ¼ miles (11.7km)	3 ½ hrs	1,145ft (350m)
The Bridestones	59	Sports Centre, Todmorden	SD 927248	7 ¼ miles (11.7km)	3 ½ hrs	1,180ft (360m)
Thurstonland, Farnley Tyas & Castle Hill	43	Brockholes Rail Station	SE 153111	5 ½ miles (8.9km)	3 hrs	1,230ft (375m)
Towneley Hall and the Singing Ringing Tree	26	Barwise, Towneley Park	SD 851306	4 ¾ miles (7.6km)	2 ½ hrs	800ft (245m)
Watergrove & Brown Wardle Hill	40	Watergrove Reservoir	SD 911176	5 ½ miles (8.9km)	3 hrs	1,000ft (305m)
Wycoller & Boulsworth Hill	89	Ball Grove Picnic Site, Colne	SD 908401	9 ¼ miles (15km)	5 hrs	1,735ft (530m)

Comments

An airy walk at one of the high passes through the Pennines, taking in a Roman Road and the superb viewpoint of Blackstone Edge.

This walk explores the hidden valleys of the Naden and Cheesden brooks, with their superb woodlands and gaunt mill remains amid stirring moorland scenery.

A challenging circuit of the moors around this striking glacial feature, visiting Thieveley Pike, an old silver mine, and an archetypal South Pennine mill village.

Pretty stone villages, great industrial heritage and tranquil countryside where the South Pennines end and the Yorkshire Dales begin beyond the Aire Valley.

Old stone quarry tramroads and cartways slink across Cowpe Moor past reservoirs and along stirring Rooley Moor Road to memorable views across the roof of England.

A beautiful, contrasting walk visiting moorland farms, hamlets and fabulous wooded gorges, with some intriguing industrial archaeology and a grand pub along the way.

An old railway and walled moorland tracks link some of the prettiest weaver's villages in the South Pennines; there's a Hollywood connection, too.

A heady mix of Brontë heritage, *Railway Children* locations and pretty sections of the little Worth Valley around the lovely town of Haworth.

Above Whitworth, paths and tracks climb to a fascinating cobbled moorland road before visiting beautiful Healey Dell, in the gorge of the River Spodden.

An idyllic wooded ghyll draws this walk up onto Ilkley Moor, a circuit of which is a transect through 7,000 years of human usage of this famous Yorkshire location.

A walk combining sublime natural and man-made attractions, from the timeless village of Heptonstall to the wooded gorge and crags of Colden Water.

A walk in a quiet corner of *Last of the Summer Wine* country, ending with a glorious wooded gorge following a moorland-edge exploration above this tranquil village.

A short and hilly walk through a lovely backwater of the South Pennines, visiting monuments on a spectacular crag above Airedale.

An energetic, linear, inter-station walk to the South Pennines' most famous viewpoint at Stoodley Pike before a final flourish down the beautiful, sylvan Cragg Vale to Mytholmroyd.

A tremendous walk exploring the moors and byways of Luddenden Dean, one of the South Pennines' greatest secrets, haunt of a Poet Laureate.

A walk beside the peaceful Rochdale Canal leads to a ramble below Stoodley Pike to Mankinholes and the remarkable waterwheel tower at Lumbutts.

A great introduction to the South Pennines, with packhorse bridges, canal heritage, milltown atmosphere and a superb moorland walk.

Moorland, wooded valleys, haymeadows and green vales enliven this easy ramble above the steep streets of Sowerby Bridge and Halifax.

This walk scurries up a miniature wooded glen before emerging onto wild moorland, dotted with wind turbines and offering great views.

There's a refreshingly remote feel to this walk on old packhorse routes and miner's tracks high above Oldham, and a handy moorland pub too.

Explore the wilder side of Brontë Country, rising to the remote Alcomden Stones, a fabulous viewpoint over the area's moorland fastness.

This walk is a challenging circuit of the vales and moors surrounding the charming old mill village of Ripponden.

High above the Aire Valley, this walk discovers picturesque, secluded mill villages, hill farms and a hidden, tranquil wooded dale.

Climbing steeply from the Calder Valley, paths snake to The Bridestones, gritstone outcrops eroded into fantastical shapes, before a tranquil, wooded return to Todmorden.

An undulating inter-station walk through the tranquil farmland and wooded vales south of Huddersfield, leading to a famous viewpoint.

A walk of contrasts, from the manicured parkland of Towneley Hall to moorland edge paths and the spectacular panopticon at Crown Point.

Watergrove is encircled by a necklace of moorland brows and flat-topped hills, great countryside for wild birds and terrific views to the distant Peak District.

The highest point of the South Pennines is the culmination of this energetic walk via the charming weaver's hamlet of Wycoller and the windy moorland of Boulsworth Hill.

At-a glance

Introduction to South Pennines

The South Pennines – an overview

Millstone Grit, a type of coarse sandstone, lies over one mile thick up the spine of England, deposited by vast river systems in huge deltas 300 million years ago. Constant erosion and weathering have honed these resistant strata into a landscape of moors, gorges, crags and vales that are the very epitome of northern England. Enriched by the built environment created during the Industrial Revolution, these skirling acres straddling the traditional boundary of Lancashire and Yorkshire and linking the Yorkshire Dales and Peak District National Parks offer an inspirational choice of walking opportunities.

The natural world

Blanket bog, cotton grass flushes, groughs, mires and carpets of heather and bilberry clothe the uplands, an ever-changing kaleidoscope of colours grazed by grouse and sheep. Around 13,000 years ago, glacial meltwaters scoured out many of the gashes and gorges that typify today's distinctive countryside, from the stark grandeur of the Cliviger Gorge to the arboreal splendour of Hebden Dale. The copious rainfall, which has nibbled at the moors to further develop these valleys is managed by utility companies; chains of reservoirs dapple the uplands enjoyed by the millions of residents of the great industrial conurbations of Lancashire and Yorkshire's West Riding. Watery glens, cascades and waterfalls were a Victorian Arcadia and remain a majestic counterpoint to the high moorlands.

The area is designated in large part as both an SSSI and a Special Protection Area due to its particular wealth of fauna and flora and exceptional geological sites. Rare birds here include merlin, golden plover, snipe and twite, nicknamed the Pennine Finch; mountain hares, which change their pelt colour to white during the winter months, are found in the south of the area, while red grouse eke-out their precarious existence amidst the heather moors across which the famous Pennine Way meanders.

The textile industry

The damp climate and inexhaustible becks and rivers combined with the geological accident of coal seams to engineer the perfect framework for industrial and commercial enterprise to take advantage of. Textiles were first manufactured on the hills before the Norman Conquest, the genesis of an industry that fundamentally shaped the history of the area, and the rest of Britain, over succeeding centuries.

The ubiquitous 'Dark, satanic mills' were the culmination of a factory system that originated as domestic, part-time working of locally produced wool, processed by farmer-weavers on handlooms, a dual-economy that had prospered since late-medieval times and saw the development of the packhorse roads that still thread the hills, moors and vales. Economies of scale and demand saw these gradually replaced by larger mechanical looms; the yeoman farmers who could afford to invest in such became the first industrial magnates, gradually usurping the small-scale home production techniques and amalgamating these family businesses into larger units. At first the new industrial concerns were built alongside the swift-flowing streams, vital for driving water wheels and turbines; it was the Pennines' lesser watercourses that saw the

Walsden

first industrialisation. This is where the more bucolic, stone-built mill ruins and remnants offer today's rambler and heritage enthusiasts such pleasure and enjoyment, places such as the Cheesden Valley.

The typical weavers' cottages, with their run of mullioned windows across the top storey to allow maximum daylight to enter, are a product of this time; this was the age of the out-worker, finishing part-worked cloth for clothiers and urban merchants – the self-employed became piece-work employees. Most can be dated between the 1600s and 1770s, closely followed by the flowering of larger loom-shops which were the pre-cursors of the full-blown mills, marking the transition between the domestic and industrial eras of textile production. They dapple the moorland edges and give hamlets and villages such as Dobcross the unique appearance that defines the area.

The advent of steam to drive machinery changed all this. Adapted from its original use in the mining industry, the guaranteed supply of power (as opposed to fluctuating supplies from water-power), fuelled by local coal, meant that ever-larger mills could now be located where transport links could be most efficiently developed – the major valleys where first the canals, then railways helped industrialists to change forever the face of the South Pennine valleys. Commercial considerations saw the Yorkshire Pennines specialise in heavy woollen products while the Lancashire side embraced the opportunities offered by imported cotton.

The great mill complexes were the powerhouses of Britain, made fortunes for industrialists, careers for politicians and were the glue that cemented the Empire together. Death of Empire and decline of textiles went hand-in-hand. Those few mills that remain are but a shadow of their hegemony, tantalising glimpses into a lost past; architectural anachronisms without which today's South Pennines would not have the same character.

Countryside in chaos

The countryside itself was changed by the development of the textile industry. The date of 1851 is commonly taken as the year when the urban population outstripped the rural population. In the first half of the 19th century thousands of upland Pennine farms and smallholdings succumbed to depopulation – Top Withins, the farmstead made famous by association with Emily Brontë, was one such. Whole hamlets were deserted and traditional farming practices declined. Today's melancholic ruined buildings, intricate tracery of collapsed walling and networks of tracks, trails and pathways recall that the greatest ever area of land under cultivation in England was in the Napoleonic wars in the early 1800s. The hay meadows and ghostly fields supplied the grain, potatoes and meat to win a war, but were unequal to the voracity of industrialisation.

The break with the countryside was irresistible, and the growth of the textile industry became self-perpetuating and unstoppable. The towns grew on the back of cloth but also as centres for technology, transport and so on. Only the workers suffered, their increasingly wretched rural background being replaced by often slave-like life in the factory system; basic rural housing replaced by the overcrowded terraces and back-to-backs.

As the countryside moved to the towns the huge mills, complex transport demands and ceaseless urban expansion resulted in a massive increase in the

The viaduct at Brownhill

demand for water. The wealthy new municipal corporations created water companies, purchased huge tracts of the moorlands and cleared these catchments of the livestock farmers who still eked out a living there, claiming that their centuries-old farming practices were an unnecessary pollutant – England's equivalent of the Highland Clearances.

Another industry that benefited was quarrying, for building stone and railway ballast in particular. Tramroads and industrial railways spread a fine web across the South Pennines, transforming the landscape and producing another fascinating facet for today's rambler to discover. Some of these upland sites – many abandoned soon after the Great War – are being rediscovered as ideal for wind-turbines, as controversial today as were those dark and satanic mills 150 years ago; Cowpe Moss is a fine example of such.

A walker's arcadia

As you walk the South Pennines you tread in the footsteps of generations who both endured and created a unique landscape, a millennium of upheavals that has bequeathed to the North a most tantalising and fascinating area to explore. This is not the England of travel posters or programmes, a green and pleasant land of rolling vales, prim villages, bucolic inns and country churches viewed through rose-tinted spectacles. It's so much more than that: a heady combination of heritage etched into the geological skeleton; of small farms with pocket-sized pastures rich with wildflowers picked out by a tracery of stone walls; of wooded dales and cloughs hidden in the hills; of hamlets and towns interlaced by causeys and tracks unchanged for centuries; of stunning views and challenging landscapes. The seemingly dour face of the gritty landscape has a soft underbelly, which, once discovered and savoured, will not readily or easily be forgotten. The South Pennines is truly an enigmatic land; the most glorious countryside sharing the same land as the country's most industrialised belt. Such uneasy bedfellows make exploring this region endlessly fascinating.

None of the walks in this guide is without a physical challenge – it's the very nature of the area; but equally none lacks rewards that far outweigh the effort involved. When the moors are fog-bound, then the cloughs and mill villages offer an alluring alternative, whilst on long summer days or crisp winter mornings the mosses and hills remain utterly peaceful despite being amid England's most concentrated urban agglomerations.

This book includes a list of waypoints alongside the description of the walk, so that you can enjoy the full benefits of gps should you wish to. For more information on using your gps, read the *Pathfinder® Guide GPS for Walkers*, by gps teacher and navigation trainer, Clive Thomas (ISBN 978-0-7117-4445-5). For essential information on map reading and basic navigation, read the *Pathfinder® Guide Map Reading Skills* by outdoor writer, Terry Marsh (ISBN 978-0-7117-4978-8). Both titles are available in bookshops or can be ordered online at www.totalwalking.co.uk

Haworth &
the Worth Valley

		GPS waypoints
Start	Haworth church	
Distance	3½ miles (5.6km)	☑ SE 029 372
		Ⓐ SE 019 375
Height gain	490 feet (150m)	Ⓑ SE 029 382
Approximate time	2 hours	Ⓒ SE 038 382
		Ⓓ SE 035 375
Parking	Main village car park next to Brontë Parsonage	
Route terrain	Mostly good footpaths and lanes	
Dog friendly	Some very difficult ladder-stiles	
Ordnance Survey maps	Landranger 104 (Leeds & Bradford), Explorer OL21 (South Pennines)	

Haworth was home to England's most famous literary family, the Brontës. The pretty little town itself, a filigree of lanes and passageways lined by cottages, houses and villas of immense character, clings to the steep valley-side between Haworth Moor and the River Worth. Starting at the parish church, where Rev. Patrick Brontë was incumbent for 41 years, the walk explores the local byways where his famous daughters took inspiration.

Right opposite the tourist information centre at the top of Haworth's main street, a cobbled lane departs beside the **King's Arms Inn**. Walk up this and you'll shortly be at the door to St Michael's & All Angels' Church; the Brontë crypt is below the pillar next to the South Chapel beside the chancel. Our path is the one for Haworth Moor, to the right of the graveyard, passing the village school where Charlotte Brontë once taught and the Parsonage itself. Beyond here the lane narrows to a path and passes behind houses before reaching a handgate into sloping pastures. Walk ahead on the causey-stone path, which direction ends at a handgate into a road; turn left and then keep right along the main carriageway at the junction

with Cemetery Road.

In 100 yds turn right on the lane for Lower Oldfield Farm. Drop down the grass-centred track and pass left of a rake of cottages to reach the farm. Enter the garden and use the deceptive ladder-stile on your left; beyond this walk down the sloping pasture beside a sunken track. Climb a stile at the slope foot and continue along the enclosed track beside the little River Worth to reach Long Bridge Ⓐ, an idyllic old packhorse bridge arching over the beck.

Cross this and turn right into a grassy cul-de-sac. Use the stile beside the right-hand gate at the end, joining a secluded footpath that largely keeps company with the Worth, tracing it downstream via several ladder-stiles to reach a double-bridge at a lane. Turn

left on the lane, which shortly commences a long, steady climb out of the valley, presently reaching a left-bend beneath a pylon **B**.

Use the narrow stile ahead beside the left-gate and walk the bottom edge of this horse pasture below the stable. At the end, 50 yds shy of the barn, use the gap-stile on your right and drop down the pasture-edge. Use another gap-stile and descend to use a stile into the garden of a house. Pass immediately left of the house and then turn left along the access road, following this through to the main road at the tall chimney. Cross straight over and take the rough lane that bends to the right behind this chimney, all that remains of one of the valley's many lost mills. Beyond a cottage it narrows to a walled ginnel and hits a T-junction of paths. Turn left and walk this old path above the woods; at a fork at the end of the woods keep ahead up the sloping way to reach a left-bend and an old iron kissing-gate on your right. Use this gate and skirt the right edge of the field to a handgate into a steep lane. Turn right and drop to Oakworth Station **C**.

The Railway Children cinema film directed by Lionel Jeffries, was made in 1970 on location in the Worth Valley between Oakworth, Haworth and Oxenhope.

Cross the level crossing and bend right along the road. Shortly, this passes beneath the loom-shed of a redundant mill and bends sharply left. Walk up to the next bend; here turn right along the rough lane at Vale Fold Cottages. At the kissing-gate beyond stables, turn left on a path signed for Ebor Lane. This lovely old track skims through woods beside Bridgehouse Beck, eventually crossing a footbridge just downstream of a huge old mill complex.

Upon reaching the road **D**, turn left across the steel footbridge bordering the old road bridge and swing right up to the main road. Turn right and walk down to the nearby Haworth Station. Use the curving footbridge across the railway here; at the far end go ahead up the wide, cobbled brow, Butt Lane. At the top cross straight over the main road into the curving end of Butt Lane below **The Fleece** pub. Continue uphill on the cobbled Main Street to gain the square at the top, where stands the tourist information centre and nearby **Black Bull Inn**.

Mankinholes & the Rochdale Canal

		GPS waypoints
Start	Lobb Mill Picnic Area, Todmorden, 1¼ miles east of Todmorden on the A646	✐ SD 955 246
Distance	4 miles (6.4km)	Ⓐ SD 965 253
Height gain	590 feet (180m)	Ⓑ SD 970 245
		Ⓒ SD 957 234
Approximate time	2 hours	
Parking	Lobb Mill Picnic Area car park	
Route terrain	Towpath, field paths, tracks and lanes	
Dog friendly	Several handgates and stiles mean some dogs may need lifting	
Ordnance Survey maps	Landranger 103 (Blackburn & Burnley), Explorer OL21 (South Pennines)	

From its summit level south of Todmorden, the Rochdale Canal eases into the landscape of the Calder Valley. This easy walk rises through woods to join a pre-turnpike roadway along the foot of the escarpment that looms above the valley, before visiting Mankinholes and passing the waterwheel tower at Lumbutts.

✐ Turn right from the car park, cross the main road and go left into Haugh Road. Cross the bridge over the little River Calder, walk up to the house and turn left beyond it onto the towpath

Lumbutts waterwheel tower

of the Rochdale Canal here at Lobb Mill Lock. The towpath threads past a cricket ground, boat-builders and beside meadows and woodland to reach Lock 14, Holmcoat Lock and bridge Ⓐ.

Cross the bridge and join the path ahead at a stile, waymarked as a route into Height Wood. This bears right and gradually winds up through these beautiful broadleaf woods, presently filtering onto a rough old lane. Continue uphill on this, rising up the wooded flank of a clough to reach a hairpin bend. Here; go ahead on the lesser track, a bridleway for Stoodley. Ford the beck and bend right, use the gate and rise up the rough track past a secluded house. Now free of the trees, views expand tremendously across the gorge of the Calder to the great moorlands marking the Yorkshire/ Lancashire borderland. Nearer to hand, the obelisk on Stoodley Pike takes the eye. Pass a junction to your left; then one to the right. Some 50 paces beyond this, turn left up the farm road, climbing easily now towards the distant monument. Walk to the right of the farmhouse and bend right on the track. Immediately after passing through the gap in the wall, use the stile on your left, climbing alongside the wall to use another stile higher up the slope **B**.

Turn right on the rough lane, known as London Road. This age-old trading route is now reborn as the Pennine Bridleway. Up to your left, the ever-present Stoodley Pike monument stands sentinel. The track eventually meets a tarred lane at the edge of the tranquil hamlet of Mankinholes. Turn left and trace the lane around bends to the entrance to the pub car park **C**.

Walk up to the **Top Brink Inn**. Look back from the top of the car park and you'll see the solid tower at Lumbutts Mill where three waterwheels worked, one above another. Beyond the inn, take

the path immediately left of Brink Top Cottage, joining a walled path. Go through a handgate and keep ahead on the partly setted path beside a wall on your left. Pass through a thin stile between tall stone posts and bear right along the signed Calderdale Way Link Path. This crosses the shoulder of a hillside and becomes a pronounced, ledged route through fallen walls before a handgate leads into an enclosed path, which drops gently to emerge into a lane beside cottages.

Walk down to the converted mill, cross the canal bridge and use the steps on the right to join the towpath. Put the canal on your right and walk through to the next bridge at Lobb Mill; here leave the canal, turn left on the lane and then right along the main road to find the car park.

Blackstone Edge & Reservoirs

Blackstone Edge & Reservoirs

		GPS waypoints
Start	The White House Inn	
Distance	5½ miles (8.9km)	SD 967 178
Height gain	390 feet (120m)	Ⓐ SD 962 194
Approximate time	2½ hours	Ⓑ SD 969 194
Parking	Public car park just downhill from the pub beside the A58	Ⓒ SD 977 180 / Ⓓ SD 972 163
Route terrain	Easy walking on moorland tracks, approaches to Blackstone Edge may be boggy in wet weather	
Dog friendly	Dogs must be kept on leads in the nesting season, March to July	
Ordnance Survey maps	Landranger 109 (Manchester), Explorer OL21 (South Pennines)	

Cross–Pennine transport is the linking theme of this easygoing, high level walk. Threading past canal-feeder reservoirs, a pack-horse road between Halifax and Rochdale climbs Blackstone Edge before a remarkable Roman road takes the walk towards the White House Inn, long a refuge on these windy heights.

Walk uphill past the **White House Inn** and continue beside the main road for another 150 yds to reach, on your left, a set of gates and a Pennine Way fingerpost. Join the reservoir access road here and pop up the embankment for good watery views across Blackstone Edge Reservoir, the first of a series flooding the nooks, crannies and hollows of Chelburn Moor and White Holme Moss. Immediately the superb views that characterise this walk draw the eye west along the upwelling of the West Pennine Moors, while to the north (ahead) the turbines at Coal Clough windfarm are silhouetted against distant Pendle Hill.

Beyond the reservoir the firm track meanders beside a goyt linking the chain of reservoirs, created to supply the Rochdale Canal. Just beyond a pond, a split in the track is reached virtually beneath a line of cables Ⓐ.

Fork right here, leaving the Pennine Way in favour of a Reservoir Circuit walk to White Holme. This soon bends right as a track beside White Holme Reservoir (on your left); remain with this waterside route to the next corner and a flat bridge Ⓑ. It's pleasant, easy walking with good views across to low rocky outcrops above White Holme Moss.

Cross the bridge and fork right, away from the water and alongside another goyt with which you keep company for the next ¾ mile. The firm track curls around the contour above the infant headwaters of Turvin Clough, which snakes its way northwards into Cragg Vale.

The track eventually reaches a tarred road; this is Turvin Road. Turn right along the road; as you reach the near corner of Blackstone Edge Reservoir, cross to the left and follow the fence (left) beneath the pylons through to the main road at the Calderdale/Rochdale boundary **C**.

(If this proves to be too boggy, simply remain on the minor road to its junction with the A58 and turn left to reach the boundary markers.)

Cross the road to use the gated track signed for Baitings Reservoir, joining the course of another catchwater drain. Remain beside this as the track narrows to a path, presently reaching a footbridge across the channel on your right. Use this and pick up a braided path that bends left, charting a route above a reedy, damp flush on your left. A gradual, easy climb up this old packhorse trail gains the ridge-top at an outcrop of rocks and a wayside stone, The Aiggin Stone, a medieval route-marker with some worn carving and a cross inscribed. On your left is a stile; use this and follow the well-walked path – The Pennine Way – up to the distant trig pillar on Blackstone Edge **D**.

From here, retrace your steps to the

Aiggin Stone and turn left alongside the fence along the remarkable, paved, Roman road. Upon reaching the point where a goyt passes beneath the track, turn right and trace the concrete channel around the hillside to return to the **White House**. ●

SCALE 1:25000 or 2½ INCHES to 1 MILE 4CM to 1KM

Ickornshaw & Earl Crag

		GPS waypoints
Start	Ickornshaw	
Distance	4¼ miles (6.8km)	SD 967 430
Height gain	850 feet (260m)	Ⓐ SD 965 420
		Ⓑ SD 985 425
Approximate time	2½ hours	Ⓒ SD 991 430
Parking	Roadside parking Holy Trinity church on Gill Lane, Ickornshaw (lanes west of Cowling off A6068)	Ⓓ SD 975 434
Route terrain	Almost entirely on good farm tracks and back lanes, with two steep, steady climbs	
Ordnance Survey maps	Landranger 109 (Manchester), Explorer OL21 (South Pennines)	

A short taste of the Pennine Way takes this walk steeply up from the deep clough of Ickornshaw Beck to a secluded valley and the very edge of the moors bordering Airedale. Here, Ickornshaw Moor ends at the fractured rocks of Earl Crag, a notable viewpoint capped by memorials and with a huge panorama stretching away towards the Yorkshire Dales and Pendle Hill as well as across the rippling grouse moors above Keighley and Haworth.

✏ Put your back to the churchyard gate and walk ahead on the lane away from this T-junction, past Townend Farm. Pass by the imposing old Wesleyan Chapel at the heart of this picturesque hamlet and walk on to cross a bridge over Ickornshaw Beck. Look left here for stone steps, signed as the Pennine Way for Colne Road, leading to a grassy path that climbs steeply up to the main road. Turn left to find, on the right, steps climbing the bank, again signed as the Pennine Way, this time for Lumb Lane. A steep field path rises to the farm buildings on the near horizon. Use the handgate into the yard and walk ahead to a higher handgate, beyond which remain on the rising, walled track. Beyond a crest this drops to reach gates and a fingerpost Ⓐ.

Leave the Pennine Way here and turn left, through a gate and along a wall-side track that drops, gradually at first, towards the out-of-the-way valley ahead. On a crest in the middle distance is the pillar of Wainman's Pinnacle, the target of this walk. To reach it, continue downhill, step over a beck at the stand of gnarled alders and go downhill to a flat bridge. Cross this and bear left up the walled track that starts to climb gently around the hillside, presently reaching a farmhouse. Turn left to gain a tarred lane at a sharp bend. From here, walk ahead up the constantly rising lane, remaining with it for ¾ mile and past several farmhouses to reach a parking area on the left, just before a wooden stable Ⓑ.

Turn left on a wall-side path to reach the pillar on its gritstone escarpment, Earl Crag, from which the ground plummets as a series of low cliffs into the deep valley of Ickornshaw Beck. Turn right around the corner of the wall here and walk the length of the fractured scarp to the distant Lund's Tower  which has a spiral staircase to the top.

Drop down the steps from Lund's Tower and walk down to the lane, along which turn left. Stay on this for nearly a mile and bend sharp right with it. At the next right-bend turn left along the drive (waymarked); in 20 paces take the handgate on the right and walk down the field past three large ash trees. At the corner, slip along a fenced ginnel to emerge on an estate road; walk past the play area to the main road .

Cross over and turn right to reach the roadway to Woodside Farm. Turn along this; at the farmyard join the sloping, cobbled path ahead down a few steps.

Wainman's Pinnacle

This becomes a peaceful streamside way, dropping to cross a footbridge before ascending a paved path towards the nearby, elevated cottage. Turn left at the retaining wall here, joining an old track, which runs via handgates to reach a stockyard. From here, walk the farm road to return to the church.

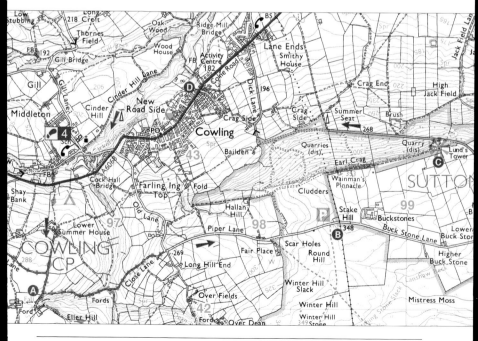

Norland Moor

			GPS waypoints
Start	Norland Moor		SE 055 218
Distance	4¾ miles (7.6km)		SE 066 223
Height gain	785 feet (240m)		SE 081 220
Approximate time	2½ hours		SE 076 213
Parking	Public car park opposite The Moorcock pub		SE 065 209
Route terrain	Sandy paths, tracks and lanes		
Dog friendly	Lots of stone slab stiles to use		
Ordnance Survey maps	Landranger 104 (Leeds & Bradford), Explorer OL21 (South Pennines)		

An easy exploration of a moorland bloc fringing the outskirts of Halifax. Ramble across the tops, enjoy great views, pleasant woodland walking and visit a superb wooded dell before winding along the flank of a tranquil green valley to return to the start.

Join the path that climbs from the back of the car park up the heathery slope. It winds through overgrown workings before reaching the lip of the slope; here turn left on the wide path along the edge of Norland Moor.

As the walk progresses, the impressive skyline of the nearby centre of Halifax takes the eye. At railings, the Calderdale Way forks off to the right, but we continue ahead on the wide path at the moorland edge. Keep slightly right beneath a line of wires, presently reaching a cross-path next to a wooden pylon about 100 yds short of a lane **Ⓐ**.

Turn right and walk through to a path junction; here go left to reach a walled corner at the moorland edge where you should step across the beck and put the wall on your right, walking through to a junction of lanes at a bridge. Go ahead up the main lane towards the nearby bungalow. Immediately before this, take the Calderdale Way to your left. Pass by a handgate on your left and remain on

the in-field path to find a wooden stile at a corner. Use this and pick up a good path through the top of the woods, remaining with this to reach a wider track at the entrance to a farmhouse drive. Bear right on the track (not the drive) and climb gently along this, past a bungalow to a cross-lane **Ⓑ**.

Go straight ahead along Moor Bottom Lane. Some 100 yds before the next farmhouse, turn right on a waymarked path, a field-side part-paved way which traces the wall on your left to and through further stiles. Cross a farm track and use a slab stile beneath a lone, stunted oak tree. Use the next slab stile and turn left, passing almost beneath a pylon and heading for the nearby farmhouse. Stiles take the path through paddocks to the right of the house before joining the driveway. Where this kinks left in 250 yds, use the two close-spaced stone stiles on the right and walk through the concreted farmyard to gain Turbury Lane. Turn left to the main

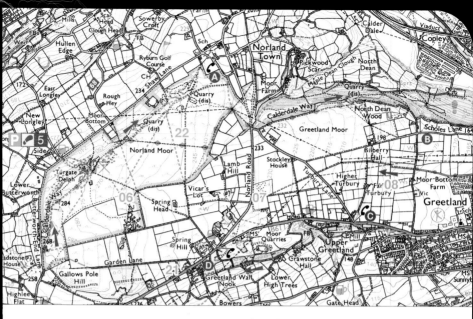

0	200	400	600	800 METRES	1	
						KILOMETRES
						MILES
0	200	400	600 YARDS	½		

road at Upper Greetland **C**.

Turn right and cross the road. Immediately past the first house, turn left down the concrete driveway, from which a narrow path keeps ahead and then right, cutting below gardens below a retaining wall to enter a peaceful wooded dell. Go straight over a falling cross-track, dropping to cross a nearby slab footbridge and then rising on a muddy path that bends right at the edge of the woods. On reaching the driveway at the old Crawstone Hall, turn right to a nearby wider tarred lane and go left on this. At the point this swings left beyond a white-painted cottage, fork right on a rougher track and walk this beside the lovely beechwoods.

Keep ahead at the fold of cottages, passing just to the right of 'Bank End' to trace the green track through to a handgate into a horse paddock. At the far end of this, use the gate beside the water trough and look ahead to sight a handgate towards the top of the far field boundary. An awkward step here leads onto a garden path; head right of the cottage and then turn right up the path

to the right of the garage, reaching a lane **D**.

Turn left to the nearby rake of cottages on the right. A waymark points the way, right, immediately before these up a steep, stepped, concrete path, which issues into a driveway; climb this to the lane at the top. Cross straight over into the rough track beside a bus shelter. The track, Garden Lane, bends left and rises gently as a walled track, presently passing by a plantation of gnarled old oak and beech. Go through a bridlegate and rise alongside grassy pasture to a second bridlegate. Do not use this; instead look half-right for the smaller, higher fenced enclosure and aim to walk just left of this. At a walled corner just above this, use a slab stile into access land and turn right alongside the wall at the edge of Norland Moor.

As the wall turns right, keep ahead to the white-painted triangulation pillar. Go straight past this and on to the nearby rocky outcrop. Turn right on the wide path. **The Moorcock** pub soon comes into view down to your left, and you'll shortly reach a path junction where a left turn takes you back down to the car park. ●

Marsden Moor & March Haigh Reservoir

Marsden Moor & March Haigh Reservoir

		GPS waypoints
Start	The Green, Marsden, next to church	✎ SE 047 116
Distance	4¾ miles (7.6km)	Ⓐ SE 048 123
Height gain	1,000 feet (305m)	Ⓑ SE 029 126
Approximate time	2½ hours	Ⓒ SE 016 128
Parking	Ample roadside parking near the church	Ⓓ SE 028 121
Route terrain	Lanes, farm tracks, moorland paths. One steep climb	
Dog friendly	Dogs must be kept on leads on the moorland section (awkward stiles in the early stages)	
Ordnance Survey maps	Landranger 103 (Blackburn & Burnley), Explorer OL21 (South Pennines)	

This revealing walk typifies the South Pennines. From the traditional milltown of Marsden radiate packhorse trails, turnpikes, canal and railway, all redolent of the heady days of the height of the Industrial Revolution. The walk climbs onto the enfolding moors, with the reward of solitude and captivating views, all achieved on an easy circuit above the Colne Valley.

✎ From The Green, walk upstream between the churchyard wall and the River Colne (Clough Lee). In 100 yds cross the packhorse bridge and turn left to new housing. Fork right up the railed path and then across the bridge over the Huddersfield Narrow Canal and the railway here at Marsden Station. Turn right; in 30 paces go left up narrow Spring Head Lane. A steep pitch reaches a house beyond a strip of firs; pass to its left, up steps and an enclosed path and then through stiles to a rough lane near a farmhouse Ⓐ.

Turn left, pass the farm and remain with this walled track. Keep left at a fork, shortly passing remote buildings. The occasionally tarred lane passes cottages and farms; keep along the upper level at any junction. The lane reaches a fork well above a modernised farm; at this junction turn right (footpath fingerpost) and walk to secluded buildings. Take the concreted ramp right of the house, behind which a handgate gains a walled path. Another gate leads into a path rising gently to a further handgate at a crest. Go slightly right (do not cross the wooden bridge); a marker post confirms your route to and past a tumbled ruin. Fall to a flat bridge over a beck; here bend left to the sycamores, then right up to a gate Ⓑ.

Turn right along the

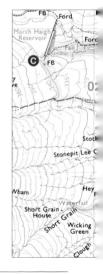

Great Edge and March Hill

clipping the top of a narrow clough before descending a second such to cross the superb Close Gate packhorse bridge 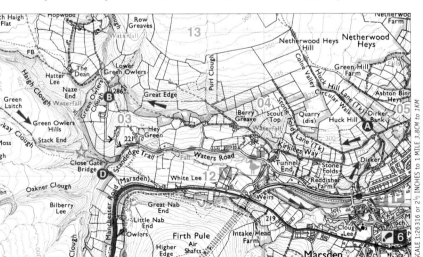.

Follow the River Colne downstream, go ahead on a lane straight over the crossroads and past a row of cottages. Slip right onto a path through a nature reserve before regaining the lane near **Tunnel End Inn**. Turn right at the inn and follow signs to the warehouse Visitor Centre, where exhibitions reveal the fascinating history of the Colne Valley, the canal and the remarkable Standedge Tunnels.

Cross the nearby canal bridge and turn left, passing opposite the Visitor Centre and beneath low rail bridges to reach Marsden Lock. Here; drop down Station Road (past **The Station** pub) to find The Green, on the right at the foot of the hill.

lane; at the fork beyond the farmhouse go left up the rougher lane. Keep left at the fork before White Hall Farm and, at the gateway on the left opposite the building, use the waymarked stile and go ahead onto the moor. A good path develops, heading for the bulbous snout of March Hill, above March Haigh Reservoir. Remain at the lip of Haigh Clough before crossing to the left-end of the dam itself C.

Walk ahead off the dam on a distinct path, rising gently towards the sharp snout of distant Pule Hill and curling to a concrete post marked 'PH Road'. Turn sharp left on this packhorse road,

Hepworth's Hidden Gem

		GPS waypoints
Start	Hepworth village	
Distance	4½ miles (7.2km)	✎ SE 163 067
Height gain	800 feet (245m)	Ⓐ SE 171 069
		Ⓑ SE 170 059
Approximate time	2½ hours	Ⓒ SE 171 053
Parking	With consideration, roadside in the village near the Butchers Arms	Ⓓ SE 158 057
		Ⓔ SE 153 059
Route terrain	Lanes, tracks and footpaths. Paths can be very muddy and slippery in Hepworth Dean	
Ordnance Survey maps	Landranger 110 (Sheffield & Huddersfield), Explorer OL1 (The Peak District – Dark Peak area)	

An undulating walk in one of the greener corners of the South Pennines' Last of the Summer Wine *country. The village of Hepworth ripples across the snout of a hill high above tributaries of the River Holme; it escaped any large-scale industrialisation and retains immense character. The walk rises to a hillside with excellent views before charting a return along a sublime wooded valley that echoes to the sound of waterfalls and waterchutes.*

✎ Put the **Butchers Arms** at your back and turn right along the main street. Just past the Sports & Social Club, take the waymarked path left down the thin pasture. Near the foot slip right over a stone stile and cross the nearby footbridge. Keep straight ahead and then go left on the sandy path. Fork right in 75 yds up an initially stepped path to the main road. Cross into Meal Hill Lane and fork right up a walled lane. At the T-junction turn right uphill to the point the tarred lane passes between stone gateposts Ⓐ.

Bear right up the rougher lane and hairpin-right; at the left-hairpin, take the bridlegate, right to join a grassy track around the flank of Cheese Gate Nab. Pass through a bridlegate near gnarled oaks, ignore a path from the right and remain on the track to a point 50 yds short of a farm hidden in trees.

Look carefully right for a thin path through bracken to wood-railed rough stone steps. Drop directly to a gate and handgate into the edge of woodland at the field-foot; bear right on the muddy track to a stile onto the main road. Turn left; then right through a handgate just before the gate-posted drive to Lower Millshaw. At the far-right corner of the paddock, use another handgate and go ahead beside a wall on your right. Just past the pond, take the slim stile on the right and turn left. Slip through the gap to put the wall on your right and walk to the distant cottages. Go left to Barnside Lane and turn right.

Opposite the last cottage on the right Ⓑ, turn left into a short entry. Climb the stile and turn left on the path. Initially beside a wall on your left, beyond a stile it strikes through tussocky pasture; further stiles draw

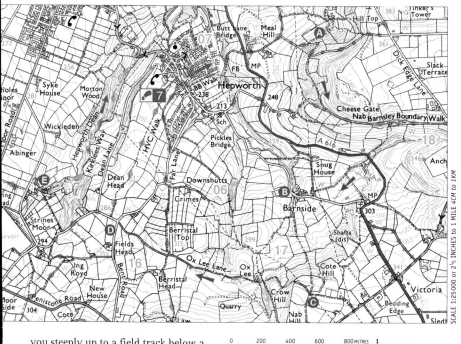

you steeply up to a field track below a line of cables **C**. Turn right, pass a length of rail fence and drop right with the rough Ox Lee Lane to reach an abandoned farm. Pass just above this (do not turn left) along the continuance of the track, now a roughly walled way, to reach a tarred cross-lane in ¹⁄₂ mile **D**.

Go ahead along Cowcliffe Hill Road, which bends left beside woods to a bridge. Immediately over this turn right on an enclosed path beside a garden to

Hepworth Dean

a stile, beyond which it remains a fenced path. More stiles take the path beside a wall on your right, down steps and round corners to a fold of cottages **E**.

Turn right along the rough track; in 20 paces look right for a waymarked flight of wooden steps down to a path beside Hepworth Dean Beck. For nearly a mile the path – *muddy and slippery underfoot, so take particular care* – accompanies the beck through a wooded dingle. Footbridges and stepping stones joust with the water; in places the streamside path is narrow, other stretches see it well above the valley floor. At the lane turn right and walk uphill. Just as the road reaches the bus-turning area at the edge of Hepworth, turn sharp right on Dean Lane. In 75 yds take the waymarked path left, which cuts through to one of the rough back lanes in the old part of the village. Keep ahead to find the **Butchers Arms**.

Towneley Hall and the Singing Ringing Tree

		GPS waypoints
Start	Towneley Park	✏ SD 851 306
Distance	4¾ miles (7.6km)	Ⓐ SD 843 308
Height gain	800 feet (245m)	Ⓑ SD 839 297
Approximate time	2½ hours	Ⓒ SD 851 289
Parking	Barwise car park, Towneley Park, Burnley, beside the A671	Ⓓ SD 862 300
Route terrain	Generally easy going on paths and tracks, it may be marshy for a short distance after Crown Point	
Dog friendly	Agile dogs should be able to use the stiles and gates	
Ordnance Survey maps	Landranger 103 (Blackburn & Burnley), Explorer OL21 (South Pennines)	

From the woodlands above medieval Towneley Hall, this walk climbs gently to moorland edge paths and the Crown Point viewpoint high above the town. Close by here is one of East Lancashire's remarkable panopticons, the Singing Ringing Tree, an inspiring creation celebrating, through the medium of art-installation sculpture, the revival of this part of the South Pennines. The walk returns via sheep-pastures and the landscaped, manicured acres of the Towneley Hall estate.

✏ Walk up the drive back to the main road and cross into the lay-by opposite. At the right-hand end of this, a Burnley Way waymarker post points the way as left up the driveway. Go through the gate into the woods and keep ahead to a path junction just before the woodland edge. Turn right and then fork left on the path that skims the top end of the woodlands. Scattered throughout the woods, but difficult to identify, are the remains of 70 beehive coke ovens built in Victorian times.

At the end of the woods use the stile into a sloping meadow and head right on a good path that ends at a stile into a rough lane. Turn left on this; in 100 yds,

at the heart of the pretty dell, turn left (before the beck) and then take the left-hand, gated path up the slope. In a further 100 yds take the right fork, shortly climbing steps to reach the main road Ⓐ.

Turn left and walk 50 yds before crossing to use the waymarked drive opposite. In just a few paces slip right onto an enclosed, waymarked path, climbing this to a stile, then beyond up the left-edge of the pasture. This path passes above a beck on your left and then joins a gravelled driveway; head up this and pass to the right of the buildings, continuing up the hard-surfaced track. Slip left of the covered reservoir to reach a stile at the edge of a golf course. Go straight ahead across two fairways before following the marked path through a young copse, pass left of the old farmhouse and then slip right through a screen of trees. Turn left beside the drain bridged by ornate bridges and simply head uphill across further fairways; a distinct hollow way takes you to the top boundary wall and a stile, turn left here towards the nearby road junction **B**.

Look on your left just shy of the junction for a stile and a 'Walkers Welcome' disc. Join this path, which heads into immature mixed woodland, part of the Burnley Millennium Forest. Waymarked as the Copy Clough Walk, the path meanders through the trees, barely losing much height and staying roughly parallel to the road off to your right. On reaching a waymarked post on

an obvious dyke, turn right for 40 yds and then fork left on a walked path that starts to gain height out of the woods. Your target is in sight, the odd-looking structure on the nearby hilltop; simply follow the paths to reach the car park here at Crown Point and then turn left on the wide, fenced path to reach the Singing Ringing Tree **C**.

This panopticon is shaped as a tree twisting away from the wind; made from hollow tubes, the wind often causes it to emit a low hum. The sculpture is inspired by the enchanted tree, which featured in a 1960s television series loosely based on a Brother's Grimm fairytale. The views from this location are superb, especially north to the Yorkshire Dales, Bowland

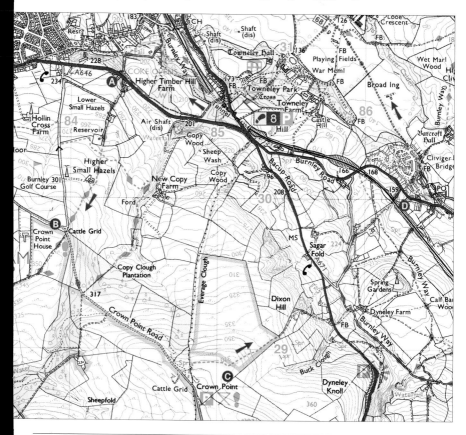

The Singing Ringing Tree Panopticon

and nearby Pendle Hill.

Use the stile out of the enclosure (on the right as you approached) and turn downslope over reedy pasture, parallel to a wall on your right. Cross a stile and continue downhill, aiming just left of the cottage to find a stile onto the tarred driveway; walk down to the main road. Cross this and turn right a few paces to a waymarked stile on the left; drop down the steps and walk down beside the right edge of the deep, wooded gully to a stile and steps onto a farm lane at Dyneley Cottage. Turn left to a junction, here bear right and trace this narrow road to a small wood in 500 yds. Look carefully on the right here for a Burnley Way fingerpost indicating the route across a footbridge (not up the drive), keep the estate wall on your right and, beyond a stile, drop to use a hand-gated crossing of the railway line. The main road is just below this **D**.

Look right for a waymarked path on the left and follow this between housing, across an estate road and ahead above the infant (Lancashire) River Calder to reach a footbridge. Do not cross this but bear left to regain a road. Turn right; then first right along Broad Ing Close. At the T-junction go left and use the handgate beside a metal gate, giving access to the estate at Towneley Hall. Keep ahead beside the fence, presently reaching a handgate into a large mown meadow area. Turn left and shortly bear right along the woodland edge. Use the steps on the left at a bridge and turn right along the woodland path at one of the inventive sculptures on the sculpture trail here.

You'll shortly reach Towneley Hall, the ancestral home of the Towneley Family, whose members still rank highly in Lancashire society. It was purchased by Burnley Council in the 1900s opening as a public museum and park. The Hall (entry fee, closed Fridays) contains much period furniture, glass, ceramics, sculpture and a fine array of Victorian paintings in the town's Art Gallery here.

Find the front of the Hall (not the side with the fountain and lake); from here a tarred driveway climbs an avenue of huge lime trees to reach a memorial cross, Foldy's Cross. Bear half-right from this to the nearby car park. ●

Cheesden Valley

		GPS waypoints	
Start	Ashworth Moor Reservoir	🖋 SD 829 160	
Distance	6½ miles (10.5km)	Ⓐ SD 840 149	
Height gain	770 feet (235m)	Ⓑ SD 845 143	
Approximate time	3 hours	Ⓒ SD 854 142	
Parking	Off-road parking opposite Owd Betts pub at Ashworth Moor Reservoir, on A680 between Rochdale and Edenfield	Ⓓ SD 853 135	
		Ⓔ SD 840 133	
		Ⓕ SD 829 136	
		Ⓖ SD 824 145	
		Ⓗ SD 820 154	
Route terrain	Farm tracks, lanes and field paths, may be very muddy in places		
Dog friendly	Some very difficult ladder-stiles		
Ordnance Survey maps	Landranger 109 (Manchester), Explorers OL21 (South Pennines) and 277 (Manchester & Salford)		

High up in the moors above Rochdale are secluded wooded gorges which once hummed with the sounds of modest textile mills; the gaunt remains of such add a melancholic air to this adventurous walk which threads along the sylvan valleys, past millponds and through relict communities in a beautiful, austere countryside where wind turbines now harvest a different natural resource.

🖋 Walk away from **Owd Betts**, with the reservoir on your right. In 200 yds bear right on a path past the renovated reservoir house and cross tarred Ashworth Lane into a boggy track. Pass the farmhouse and walk the drive towards the road. Turn right on the signed bridleway, shortly descending a walled track to reach a lane. Keep ahead past the houses and bend left to a nearby junction Ⓐ.

Turn right to the fold of cottages. Take the handgate beside the farthest, white-painted farmhouse and go left on the enclosed track, through a gate and along the Rochdale Way over two stiles. Turn right beyond the small fenced area on a path that becomes a dirt track, then a path along the edge of a wooded clough.

Where the clough turns right at a stand of beech Ⓑ, look left for the distant cottage; a stiled path heads to this. Pass to its immediate left and slip right through the farmyard before the barn, joining the rough access lane. Cross the cattle-grid beyond the second gate and bend left through the clough; pass **Millcroft Tearoom** and remain on the lane to reach pretty Wolstenholme Fold.

Fork to the right of Schofield Farm Ⓒ and drop into the woodlands of Naden Brook. The ruins of old textile mills litter the valley floor; the brick chimney is a local landmark. Cross Paper House footbridge and turn left. At the nearby junction, favour the middle option, rising to join a path within the woodland edge above the gorge.

At School Lane Ⓓ turn right to the

T-junction. Turn left, then right over a gate-side stile in 40 paces. At the sharp bend in the track, leave it and walk ahead, fence on your left. At the far end, use the stile just up from the corner and go ahead (not half-right) along the right-edge of the lower, flatter ground. This pasture narrows to a point above the woodland edge and a stile; keep ahead up a narrow field, at the left corner a cattle path forks ahead-left beside a fence, dropping into the wooded clough. It's awkward underfoot; you'll presently reach a place where stones make crossing the beck easy. Turn back-left on a narrow path up old wooden steps. At the crest look left for a handgate; join the path down to cross a footbridge in a glade, bear right along the wide path, then left up to a lane near a secluded house. Walk uphill to a barrier in 150 yds.

Take the waymarked stile **E**, right, onto a path along the foot of haymeadows. After further stiles this path becomes a narrow ledge along the lip of the Cheesden Gorge. At a junction of paths at manhole covers, keep ahead on the thin, rising way to reach a moorland road near a gateway **F**.

Turn right and trace this level track gradually left. When a house is visible below, drop right on a braided path to join a wall on your left. Your target is the stone chimneystack on the valley floor: a good path leads towards this, which marks the site of Washwheel Bleachworks, the last of the mills to close in this lonely valley in 1919. About 100 yds before the chimney, fork left up the middle track, lined by hawthorns. This runs along the valley edge before, beyond stone gateposts, dropping into woodland. Here are the tumbled remains of Deeply Vale Printworks, where calico was processed; an incongruous cobbled track leads to

the large millpond. Turn right across the dam and then left along a wide track **G**.

Continue through a flat area where terraces of housing and mill buildings once stood, all abandoned in the late 1800s. Pass left of a lake, up a bank and left via a stile along the cindered track to the T-junction. Turn right to the dormer-windowed old Buckhurst School. Keep right here; at the nearby junction go right onto a rough track and immediately use the stone gap-stile on the right. **H** Turn left and in a few paces keep right on a narrow, flagged

path beneath alders to pick a way along the left-edge of the reedy valley floor. Stay with this for 550 yds, cross the low double bridge, pass the waterfall and trace the path ahead to the imposing ruins of Cheesden Lumb Woollen Mill, spanning Cheesden Brook and which closed in the 1890s.

Cheesden Valley

Use the concrete footbridge and kissing-gate behind the mill and walk the marshy path to a division in 200 yds; keep right to reach steps and a handgate through the retaining wall of the main road here. Turn right for **Owd Betts**.

Ogden Reservoir, Nab Hill & Ovenden Moor

Start	Ogden Reservoir
Distance	6 miles (9.7km)
Height gain	620 feet (190m)
Approximate time	3 hours
Parking	Car park signposted off A629 between Halifax and Keighley; turn off at the Causeway Foot Inn along Ogden Lane
Route terrain	Woodland and moorland paths, tracks, back lanes
Dog friendly	Agile dogs only, keep on lead in Nature Reserve and between March and July. There are cattle-grids
Ordnance Survey maps	Landranger 104 (Leeds & Bradford), Explorer OL21 (South Pennines)

GPS waypoints

- 🖉 SE 065 309
- Ⓐ SE 053 317
- Ⓑ SE 047 329
- Ⓒ SE 035 327
- Ⓓ SE 045 306
- Ⓔ SE 058 306

An enchanting miniature glen is the precursor to some superb upland walking on the tops high above Halifax. Great views abound; the route encounters old and new moorland industries and offers a wealth of water, woodland and upland birdlife.

🖉 Locate the information board at the rear of the lower car park and use the handgate, dropping on a railed path to a junction. Turn right, on the Woodland Trail above Ogden Reservoir, falling to a reservoir-side path. Turn right to the long causeway bridge on your left. Do not cross this; instead slip ahead on a narrow path beside a wall (left), rising to a wider path along which bear left. A woodland path traces the beck up a steep-sided cleft in the moorland's edge.

At the end of the woods, go left on the path for Ogden Clough & Waterfalls. There are some superfluous footbridges, just favour the right-bank past lively falls in this lovely glen to a curving stone dam across the head of the valley Ⓐ.

Turn right for Thornton Moor and climb the flight of steps to a bridlepath. Turn left by a bench and walk the wide, braided track above the crags. In 500 yds the track forks away from the beck; bear right along the braided way across the moor – if you reach a fence across the beck you've gone 200 yds too far. This wide path undulates gently across the tops; wind turbines are now constant companions off to your left.

Cairns guide you across the moor, with terrific views across

Thornton Moor Reservoir towards Bradford and the Aire Valley. A fence appears to your left; accompany this for 200 yds to reach a kissing-gate through it **B**.

Use the gate and pick up a distinct path cutting across a moorland corner; pass through a tumbled wall and bend left on this widening way. The path snakes through the melancholic workings of small quarries and across the head of deep cloughs, drawn to the distant stone structures on Nab Hill **C**.

Beyond the imposing shelter here the path threads through further delphs (workings) before curving downhill to a tarred lane. Turn left along this crumbling old moorland road, with great views across gently rolling moorland into Lancashire. Near to hand is Warley Moor Reservoir, also known as Fly Flatts. Past the entrance to the sailing club, the first moorland farms come into view and shortly a car park

and wind-farm viewing area is passed. Remain on the lane to the first building on the left, which was, until recent closure, the highest pub in the West Riding, Withens Hotel **D**.

Turn left along the front of the building to a gate into a bridleway. Walk this wide, stony track to reach a woodland nature reserve on your left and a golf course.

Just past the 13th tee, use the stile on your left **E** into a narrow path beneath pines. This meets a gravely path, along which turn right, dropping to a wider path. Cross straight over to reach another narrow path parallel to a wall; turn right to another wider path and a nearby wall-gap onto a reservoir-side track. Turn right, cross the dam and walk past the visitor centre, beyond which bear left to the car park. ●

| 0 | 200 | 400 | 600 | 800 METRES | 1 | |
| 0 | 200 | 400 | 600 YARDS | ½ | | KILOMETRES MILES |

SCALE 1:26316 or 2½ INCHES to 1 MILE 3.8CM to 1KM

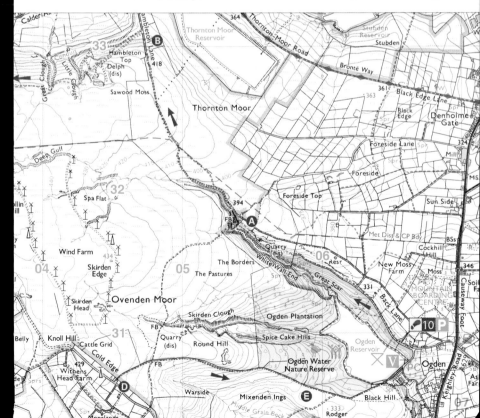

Healey Dell

		GPS waypoints	
Start	Broadley Old Station		
Distance	5½ miles (8.9km)	🔲	SD 879 164
Height gain	885 feet (270m)	Ⓐ	SD 880 168
		Ⓑ	SD 879 175
Approximate time	3 hours	Ⓒ	SD 876 174
Parking	Healey Dell Nature Reserve car	Ⓓ	SD 863 180
	park, Station Road, Broadley	Ⓔ	SD 871 158
		Ⓕ	SD 881 151
Route terrain	Mostly good paths and tracks, but about 1 mile of rough moorland paths		
Dog friendly	Stiles and ladder-stiles make the going tough		
Ordnance Survey maps	Landranger 109 (Manchester), Explorer OL21 (South Pennines)		

The serene woodlands and waterfalls of wildflower and bird-rich Healey Dell Nature Reserve are the culmination of this short exploration of a cradle of the Industrial Revolution, where medieval 'outworking' practices gave way to early mill complexes. Tracks rise easily to the fringes of Rooley Moor, offering tremendous views across both the Manchester Basin and the South and West Pennine Hills.

The car park stands amid the scant ruins of Broadley Wood Mill, opened just after Waterloo and closed after the First World War; a board details its chequered history.

🖌 Opposite the entrance to the car park, a ramped and stepped path drops to the nearby old railway line, along which turn left. In spring the cutting and ponds here are a riot of colour, with the River Spodden off to the right adding its watery tones. Remain on the old track to reach a gate and handgate across the way just past a footbridge. Just beyond this, turn left Ⓐ along the widest path. This area of alder and willow disguises the site of a stone rubbing mill, where rough stone slabs were dressed before onward transport by rail to be used as roofing and paving throughout Britain. This stone was

moved from quarries on the moors on a tramroad, the route of which is joined for a short while before a T-junction is reached.

Turn right and walk this rough lane; turn left at the junction just before houses and follow the track to a point 30 paces before a gate closes the track. Turn right on a wide path here, rising to continue on a fenced path between haymeadows and housing. Keep ahead as a farm lane joins from the left, and ahead again past garages and a road from the right. The track narrows to a path and reaches newly built, light-stone houses Ⓑ. At this point turn left and climb the slabbed, field-side path with a wall on your right. Go ahead along the drive at the top before skimming immediately right of the house to find a farm lane. Turn left and

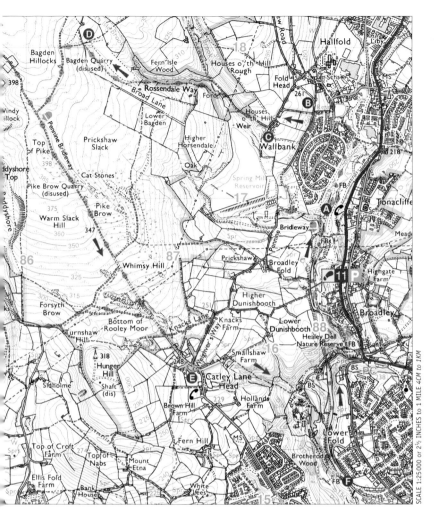

SCALE 1:25000 or 2½ INCHES to 1 MILE 4CM to 1KM

walk past barns and outbuildings to reach a gate, beyond which Spring Mill Reservoir is visible.

Take the waymarked stile on the right **C** joining a path beside a high wall (left). The path reaches a stile into access land before dropping ahead right to a footbridge below a distant tree. Cross the bridge, scramble steeply up ahead for a few yards and then bear right on the rising path which charts a ledged way above a beautiful, deep wooded clough on your right. Stick with the path near the edge, use a handgate and continue uphill, aiming for the grassy knolls, which mark the

location of Bagden Quarry. It was from here that stone was lowered by tramroad to the railway at Broadley. You should aim ahead along the left edge of the narrowing old workings, working a way up to a ladder-stile in a boggy corner by a length of vaccary fencing (upright stone slabs) **D**.

Climb the stile and walk ahead in the direction shown by the arrow; it's a boggy, tussocky way that reaches the line of an old moorland road in about 200 yds. Turn left on this and start a splendid, airy walk across the edge of Rooley Moor, with excellent views to accompany the sound of curlew, skylark and wheatears. On reaching a wider roadway turn left. This is the southern section of the remarkable, cobbled Cotton Famine Road, built as a work-creation project in the 1860s *(see Walk 23 Cowpe Moss & the Famine Road)*. Wind turbines dot the moors, while views open out west to the shadowy hills of mid-Cheshire and distant north Wales. Stay on this old road to reach the hamlet of Catley Lane Head.

Cross the cattle-grid and turn left along Smallshaw Road **E**. Enter the farmyard and turn right (signed) in front of the barn, then left alongside it to reach a gate and gap-stile. Turn right through this alongside a rotting wooden fence; the path drops into woodland, at a small clearing in 150 yds fork right on a path down to cross an old bridge and walk the meandering path above the beck. Skirting the edge of a large clearing, keep ahead-left, dropping to cross a metal footbridge before rising past cottages to a lane. Turn right to walk between the remaining buildings of the old mill complex here – corn

mills first harnessed the waters of the River Spodden in medieval times, while the Second World War saw a secret munitions factory located in this hidden valley. The Nature Reserve Information Centre here helps set the local scene.

Walk up the lane to a set of huge concrete bollards on your right **F**; here turn back left on a path which rises to join the old railway. Keep ahead to reach the viaduct over the gorge: a great vantage point high above the woods of Healey Dell Nature Reserve. Return off the viaduct and take the steps, left, down to a lane. Pick up the path opposite left, which drops right, into the woodlands of the Nature Reserve. Tumbled ruins evidence 'Th' Owd Mill i' t' Thrutch' ('thrutch' is local dialect for a 'gorge') that once stood here amid a series of waterfalls. The stepped path rises beside the Fairies Chapel through magnificent beechwoods. In time, a side path diverges to a viewing platform over the lively shoots and falls, while the main path rises to join Station Road; turn left to the car park.   ●

Footbridge across Prickshaw Brook

Heptonstall & Colden Clough

		GPS waypoints
Start	Heptonstall village centre	
Distance	5½ miles (8.9km)	📷 SD 986 280
Height gain	1,145 feet (350m)	**Ⓐ** SD 976 291
		Ⓑ SD 959 290
Approximate time	3 hours	**Ⓒ** SD 953 285
Parking	Small central car park, or at the	**Ⓓ** SD 962 282
	sports field along Valley View	**Ⓔ** SD 978 281
	Road/Acres Lane, 400 yds south	**Ⓕ** SD 981 282
	of the centre	
Route terrain	Lanes and tracks; field and woodland paths, muddy in places	
Dog friendly	There are steep, unprotected drops beside narrow paths, a cattle-grid and some awkward stiles	
Ordnance Survey maps	Landranger 103 (Blackburn & Burnley), Explorer OL21 (South Pennines)	

Heptonstall is one of the Pennines' prosaically perfect villages; cobbled lanes, gritstone cottages, ginnels and an evocative ruined church. Wonderfully situated on a high promontory above deep, wooded valleys created by glacial meltwater serrating the high reaches of Calderdale, grand walks radiate out onto the moorland and into the tranquil countryside. This route offers marvellous views over this tumultuous landscape, culminating in an exploration of Colden Clough, the industrial heritage of which is crumbling comfortably into the thick woodlands, and a magnificent endpiece along the crags hanging above this wooded chasm.

📷 From the village centre walk up Northgate, putting the **Cross Inn** on your immediate left. The lane shortly passes (on your right) steps down to the world's longest-established Methodist Chapel, an octagonal building completed in 1764 and where the movement's founder, John Wesley, preached. Remain with the lane, which soon bends left to a T-junction; turn right on the rough Townfield Lane to

the gate at the end. Go ahead to two ruinous gates; use the left one and head half-left on a field path that strikes across haymeadows to a road. Turn left; in about 40 paces take the narrow stile on the right and bear left, joining a path that hugs the lip of the spectacular wooded gorge of Hebden Dale, sometimes in the trees, sometimes not. *(N.B. there are very steep drops here.)*

Pass by one waymarked footpath to

the left to reach a second about 100 yds beyond power cables, marked by a low post with several waymark discs. Turn left for a few paces here; then use the small stone stile into a field corner on your right. Walk along the field foot, then just within the woods to reach a short flight of stone steps. Turn left off the foot of these and, in 100 yds, look up left for a junction of walls at the edge of the woods **A**.

Use the stile here and walk up the edge of pastures, reaching a road amid houses. Cross straight over onto the grassy Popples Common and walk near the right edge to a fork; here keep ahead, climbing gently to a fingerpost near a walled corner just a few paces shy of another tarred lane. Views south encompass Stoodley Pike and the vast moorland bloc beyond. Here turn right along the rough track for Heptonstall Moor and keep left at a fork, cross a cattle-grid and continue to the isolated house. Just before this, drift ahead right on a walled track, go through a gate and drop diagonally left across the rough area to a small handgate in the bottom-right corner. Bear right from this along a green field road; beyond a gate fork left and pass in front of the small stone barn before continuing on a steep track down to a lane. Turn right and walk this peaceful byway for 400 yds.

Fork left down the lane signed as the Pennine Bridleway **B** and drop down into the secluded valley of Colden Water. Cross a narrow bridge before forking ahead left up the roadway to Land Farm Gardens. The bridleway curls left around the boundary, then right and through three gates to reach a cross-lane above an old stone farmhouse and pond **C**. Turn left on this winding lane and enjoy a peaceful stroll along a typical open South Pennine farming valley dappled with solid farmhouses

and yeoman's halls – note the arched old packhorse bridge down to your left – presently reaching the hamlet of Jack Bridge and the **New Delight Inn D**, which has a microbrewery.

Walk uphill and fork first left along the lane marked as the Pennine Bridleway for Callis Bridge. At the next junction keep ahead, then go ahead again as the lane roughens. Cross the Pennine Way and remain on the track as it descends into the thick woodlands clothing Colden Clough. The deep valley once thrummed with the sound of mills: all are now long-closed. In $^{2}/_{3}$ mile another wide track joins from the left **E**. Turn back along this to descend to the valley bottom and a bridge at Lumb. Cross this, but before doing so divert upstream a short distance to the remains of one of the old mills: tumbled walls, flags and a huge chimney at a secluded glade beside falls and shoots.

Walk up the cobbled way beyond the bridge; turn sharp left in front of tall houses and then sharp right up the steep track, superb views opening out into the

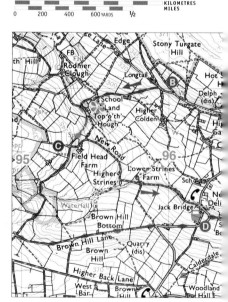

wooded gorges of Calderdale. The track becomes tarred. At a point just before a left bend at the hill crest, fork right through a gap in the wall, a path signed to Heptonstall **F**. The path skims through the edge of the woods as a challenging route across boulders and roots; in 100 yds fork left at a low waymark post, up a few natural steps and then along a path that stays near the top of the woods (do not drop down into the woods here). The path remains difficult underfoot until you pass left of a perched boulder, after which it matures as a firm way above the trees. At an offset walled corner the path thins and becomes an adventurous way at the very lip of the gorge – *take great care as there are precipitous, unfenced drops here above Hell Hole rocks.*

At a walled corner turn left on the enclosed path through a new housing development; keep ahead across estate roads, shortly reaching the old part of

Colden Clough from Lump Bank

Heptonstall and the churchyard. The grave of the poet and writer Sylvia Plath is in the churchyard of the new church of St Thomas à Becket (built in the 1850s to replace the storm-ruined old church). Near the porch of the old church is the grave of David Hartley, the so-called 'King' of the Cragg Vale Coiners, hanged in 1770 for his counterfeiting exploits. ●

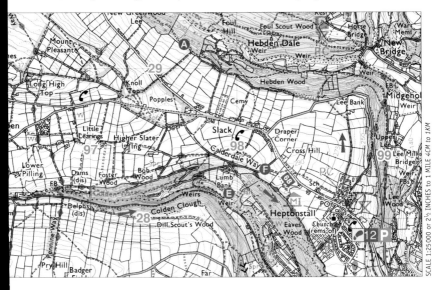

SCALE 1:25 000 or 2½ INCHES to 1 MILE 4CM to 1KM

Watergrove & Brown Wardle Hill

		GPS waypoints
Start	Watergrove Reservoir car park	
Distance	5½ miles (8.9km)	✎ SD 911 176
Height gain	1,000 feet (305m)	Ⓐ SD 913 195
		Ⓑ SD 904 196
Approximate time	3 hours	Ⓒ SD 903 195
		Ⓓ SD 892 175
Parking	Watergrove Reservoir car park, Wardle, off A58, 2 miles north-east of Rochdale	Ⓔ SD 898 165
Route terrain	Mostly tracks and old quarry roads, plus some potentially marshy paths. Waymarking in the area is poor	
Ordnance Survey maps	Landranger 103 (Blackburn & Burnley), Explorer OL21 (South Pennines)	

The South Pennines gather themselves above Rochdale as a series of flat-topped hills and moorland brows rising above steep valleys and great green embayments dotted with villages. This walk rises from the drowned settlement of Watergrove to gain the excellent viewpoint of Brown Wardle before threading back on farm tracks and haymeadows to the old mill village of Wardle.

✎ From The Trap Farm car park, named after a farm and pub that once stood on the site, climb the ramped track up to the corner of the dam and bear left, putting the reservoir on your left. The wall here incorporates date-stones from some of the farms, cottages and mills that were lost when the reservoir was created in the 1930s – some are over 300 years old. The old hamlet of Watergrove was home to over 200 souls; nothing remains of it apart from the date-stones, old tracks snaking up to the moors and tumbled ruins in the hills, de-populated to lessen the chance of pollution.

Walk the track round to the back of the former Visitor Centre (there are still interpretive boards here); here turn right up the cobbled track waymarked as the Rochdale Way. This walled old lane rises easily towards the high land that rises like a great horseshoe above the rivulets and tributaries of Higher Slack Brook, a slightly austere countryside dotted by the screes and tips resulting from quarrying and small-scale drift-mining that once employed dozens in these inhospitable acres. Passing through a gate, the track reaches a junction near the tumbled Steward Barn, marked by Pennine Bridleway signs. Bear right here, remaining on the old quarry track, which continues to climb gently through the melancholic landscape. Beyond a second gate stay with the track for 200 yds to reach a waymarked junction Ⓐ.

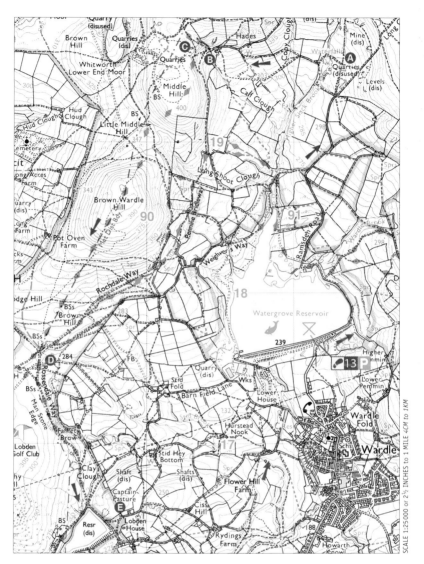

SCALE 1:25000 or 2½ INCHES to 1 MILE 4CM to 1KM

Turn left on the good cross-track which charts a level route through this uncompromising terrain, presently passing the ruins of Lower Hades Farm, on your left just past a spoil heap, to arrive at a distinct, if small, level platform about 150 yds farther on. Bend right here, putting a clough on your left and climb the dirt track to reach, on your left, the tumbled ruins of Upper Hades Farm **B**.

Pass through these ruins; immediately above them, on the left, use the stile and adjacent sleeper bridge and walk ahead on the path up through marshy terrain, bending a shade right to rise up the distinct sunken path to reach the crest of the rise amid small, domed spoil heaps. Looking back, the great green embankment is liberally dotted with old workings linked by overgrown tracks and tramroads indistinguishable from such, beyond which wave-after-wave of moorland tops take the eye. Turn left on a firm track that bends slightly right to a meeting of rough ways **C**.

Turn left, putting a shallow old quarry working on your right, while on your left steep slopes plunge down towards the lower lands above Watergrove Reservoir. The track becomes more of a moorland path across Middle Hill, with views to the right across to Knowl Hill Wind Farm, the huge Britannia Quarries and the deep valley where stands the long village of Whitworth. As the view ahead is filled by the next summit, Brown Wardle Hill, simply choose a way down the steep hillside into the col and then steeply up the other side on the braided path to gain the plateau of Brown Wardle. A line of stone posts, borough boundary markers, indicates the direction you now need to follow; essentially straight ahead towards the distant, white-walled golf course clubhouse. Ahead there are great views stretching across the Manchester Basin to the Peak District's hills and the flat Cheshire Plain.

You'll reach a meeting of tracks and lanes **D**, before reaching the golf course. A fingerpost stands here beside the only tarred lane; you should take the rough lane signed as a bridleway for Syke, putting the golf course to your right and a line of cables on your left. Walk this track through to the near corner of Brown House Wham Reservoir. Keep ahead with a wall on your right; as the track starts to descend, fork left on a rougher track that works through to a cattle-grid on a tarred lane, signed for Springside Farm **E**.

Cross the grid and walk the short distance to find a rough, fenced track forking off to the right. Take this and walk it to Ciss Hill Farm. Continue down the surfaced lane, past Rydings Mount to reach a fork, left, into the farmyard at Rydings Farm. Walk through the farmyard and between the barns, continuing beyond a gate on an enclosed track. Climb the gate-side stile and bend left with the field track to use another gate-side stile. Keep ahead beside the wall and turn left with it to a higher corner; turn right to reach the line of vaccary (stone slab) fence striking down the hillside. Turn down this to find a small handgate; use this and head across the hay meadow towards the cottages. Use another small, tight, handgate, cross the slab bridge and rise to a stile into a rough lane at the fold of cottages. Turn right and walk this through to the village square in Wardle, with its impressive chapel and the **Globe Inn**. Turn left up the lane, which shortly becomes cobbled, to return to the car park. ●

The old cobbled lane to the moor

Thurstonland, Farnley Tyas & Castle Hill

Start	Brockholes Railway Station	
Finish	Berry Brow Railway Station – regular daily trains link these stations ⓔ	
Distance	5½ miles (8.9km)	
Height gain	1,230 feet (375m)	
Approximate time	3 hours	
Parking	Brockholes Station	
Route terrain	Lanes, tracks and good field paths. Several short but steep climbs	
Dog friendly	Two awkward ladder-stiles	
Ordnance Survey maps	Landranger 110 (Sheffield & Huddersfield), Explorer 288 (Bradford & Huddersfield)	

GPS waypoints

✎ SE 153 111
Ⓐ SE 165 097
Ⓑ SE 162 114
Ⓒ SE 164 127
Ⓓ SE 151 139
Ⓔ SE 137 138

The Penistone Line railway linking Huddersfield with Sheffield threads along the pretty Holme Valley and offers many opportunities to discover the bucolic, undulating countryside of dairy farms and haymeadows. This station-to-station walk rises easily from the valley via characterful stone villages, tranquil farmland and old broadleaf woods to the superb viewpoint of Castle Hill, a commanding site which has been exploited since Roman times to control the several routes through the South Pennines here.

✎ The path from the platform at Brockholes Station drops to a road, turn left to reach a main road and go right down this. Just round the sharp right bend, cross to the left and then turn left at the War Memorial up Oakes Lane. This rises steadily before bending left into the near end of Birch Park cul-de-sac. Look right to the turning area where a fingerpost offers a choice of paths. Use the one to the right; initially an enclosed path behind gardens, which soon matures as a very old sunken path beneath bowers of holly. Upon reaching the tarred driveway; turn left and walk through to the main road. Head uphill and round the left bend to reach, on your right, the driveway to Bankside Farm. Join this and, where the tarred drive sweeps through gates, keep ahead on the path beside a wall, an elevated way offering fine views across the well-wooded countryside that characterises the Holme Valley and its tributaries. The path presently widens to a green lane and reaches a gate on the left Ⓐ, behind which is an old stock-pen (if you've reach a tarred lane you've gone

70 yds too far).

Use the gap-stile beside this gate and join the wide path, which strikes diagonally up the steep hillside through stands of gorse and scrub-birch to reach the lip of the slope. Pause here to take breath and drink in the extensive prospect across a series of low ridges and wooded valleys; Holmfirth stands at the head of one of these vales, behind which the land rises to Black Hill and Saddleworth Moor, the northern moors of the Peak District's Dark Peak. Use the ladder-stile on your right and fade a shade right to a higher ladder-stile. Once over this walk ahead with the wall/fence on your right. The moorland views are lost, replaced by a very traditional English landscape of haymeadows, pastures and pocket woods. Off to your right rises the gigantic transmitter at Emley Moor while ahead the village of Thurstonland beckons.

The wall-side path leads through

Hayrick at Thurstonland

stiles to gain the village at a lane. Turn right to the nearby main village road. Just ahead, at the crest, is the **Rose & Crown Inn**; the walk, however, crosses the road directly over into a fold of renovated farm buildings – there's a footpath fingerpost here. Walk to the right of 'The Barn' and then left along the track, which bends right, keeping left of a wall and high above a pond. An open gateway leads into haymeadows; simply keep ahead, using stiles and wall-gaps marked by weathered white-painted arrows and essentially heading for the woodland on the distant ridge-top. At the waymarked cross-path near pylons, keep ahead beneath the wires before taking the stile on the right into a walled field road. As this turns left, slip through the gap-stile on the left and walk in-field beside the track, joining a tarred driveway away from cottages to reach a lane **B**.

Turn right and then look carefully on the left in 50 yds for the waymarked footpath up rough stone steps; this rises through a scrubby sleeve of vegetation

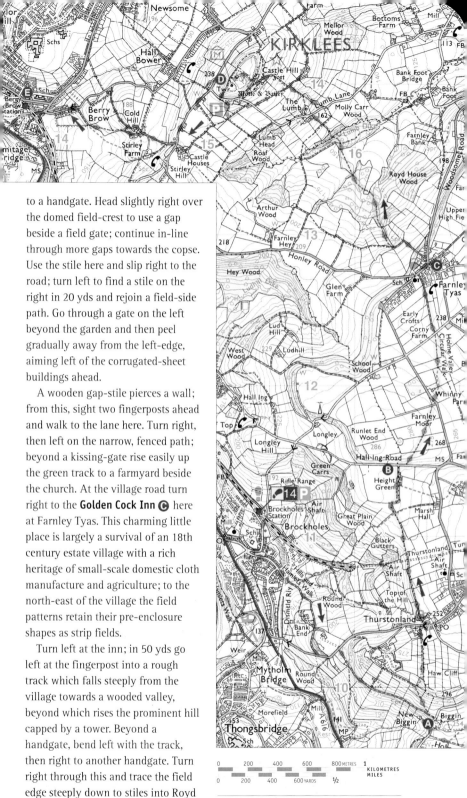

to a handgate. Head slightly right over the domed field-crest to use a gap beside a field gate; continue in-line through more gaps towards the copse. Use the stile here and slip right to the road; turn left to find a stile on the right in 20 yds and rejoin a field-side path. Go through a gate on the left beyond the garden and then peel gradually away from the left-edge, aiming left of the corrugated-sheet buildings ahead.

A wooden gap-stile pierces a wall; from this, sight two fingerposts ahead and walk to the lane here. Turn right, then left on the narrow, fenced path; beyond a kissing-gate rise easily up the green track to a farmyard beside the church. At the village road turn right to the **Golden Cock Inn** here at Farnley Tyas. This charming little place is largely a survival of an 18th century estate village with a rich heritage of small-scale domestic cloth manufacture and agriculture; to the north-east of the village the field patterns retain their pre-enclosure shapes as strip fields.

Turn left at the inn; in 50 yds go left at the fingerpost into a rough track which falls steeply from the village towards a wooded valley, beyond which rises the prominent hill capped by a tower. Beyond a handgate, bend left with the track, then right to another handgate. Turn right through this and trace the field edge steeply down to stiles into Royd

The Victoria Tower at Castle Hill

in 1897 to commemorate Queen Victoria's Diamond Jubilee. On some weekends the viewing platforms and castellation are accessible; even without this additional height, the panorama over vales and farmland to the distant moors is extensive.

Stand facing the steps leading up to the tower doorway and pass to the right of the tower's base; a steep flight of steps arrows down, crosses over a level, gravelled path around the fort ramparts and continues to the foot of the hill and a lane. Turn left, pass the lay-by and keep downhill on Lumb Lane. Take the first waymarked stile on the right, a path passing behind the white-painted house. A line of stiles takes the clear path to the farm complex in the middle distance. Looking back, Castle Hill looks like the northern sibling of Glastonbury Tor, capped with its dominating tower. Bear right through the farm on the drive passing immediately left of the right-most house here. At the lane turn right; in 30 paces go left down the surfaced track, this deteriorates to a rough lane before reaching a fold of cottages and barns.

Pass through on the now-tarred lane; just after this bends right, look left for a stile into a sloping, rough pasture. Stick to the left-edge, gradually bending right; pass through the wide gap by a dead tree and head a touch in-field, aiming directly for the blocks of flats thrusting their top storeys above the woods. Slip through the fence-gap at the fine corner of the field and turn right on an old, tree-lined track that leads through to gates and a lane by housing. Turn downhill and drop to a junction with a wider road. Turn right and cross over; take the first left, Birch Road, to find the nearby Berry Brow Station **E** – trains approaching from the left go to Huddersfield! ●

House Wood. A wide path threads through these lovely beech and oak woods, across a strip of open land and then a further finger of woodland. Use the stile at the far side and wind with a path through arable fields, bending right to reach a stile back into woodland.

Cross the bridge over a beck in this dell and rise to a stile, beyond which climb the edge of steep pastures to find a lane. Turn right and in 100 yds take the waymarked path on the left, climbing the very steep field-side path to a corner stile, then continue up the right-edge of the higher pasture to reach a rough lane. Cross diagonally left to another stile and, again, continue steeply uphill to a farther stile at the edge of a strand of scrubby bushes and trees. Walk the path, keeping straight ahead at a waymarked cross-path. Upon reaching the lane, turn right and wind round to a car park here at Castle Hill, high above Huddersfield.

D Ramparts of an Iron Age Hill Fort encircle the top of the hill, further crowned by the remains of a Norman motte-and-bailey castle and the imposing Jubilee Tower, commissioned

Piethorne Valley

Start	Newhey, Ogden Reservoir car park
Distance	5½ miles (8.9km)
Height gain	1,245 feet (380m)
Approximate time	3 hours
Parking	Off A640 Newhey to Denshaw road; look for sign to Bulls Head PH along Ogden Lane and keep left at junction along 'Private Road' to United Utilities public car park on left
Route terrain	Largely moorland tracks and paths, some possibly boggy field paths
Dog friendly	Some ladder-stiles would be very awkward for dogs
Ordnance Survey maps	Landranger 109 (Manchester), Explorer OL21 (South Pennines)

GPS waypoints

- 🖉 SD 952 122
- Ⓐ SD 948 129
- Ⓑ SD 960 133
- Ⓒ SD 977 119
- Ⓓ SD 968 111

Piethorne Clough hosts a series of reservoirs created to supply the industries and growing population of the small towns between Oldham and Rochdale. Rising along old packhorse trails, this refreshingly remote walk skirts bluebell woods and the Windy Hills – aptly named on occasion – and offers fine views across some of the highest land in the South Pennines before dropping back to the valley for a peaceful return to the hamlet of Ogden.

🖉 Turn right from the car park and right up the path onto the dam empounding Ogden Reservoir. At the far end cross the footbridge and climb up to the very narrow squeezer-stile, then turn right along the track. Pass through a gate and continue above the reedy clough to your right to reach a cul-de-sac. Use the left-hand stile and rise with the stepped path through the plantation. Upon entering Access Land at the top of the woods, continue uphill along the right-edge of the field, climbing to a stile on the horizon Ⓐ.

Turn right across another stile and join the route of a walled track, one of many former packhorse trails across the

hills hereabouts. This one also served the smattering of small-scale coalmines (there's a capped shaft on your right) and quarries in the area. At nearby Tunshill Quarry a silver arm, of Roman origin, was found in 1793. Part of a large statuette, it was possibly the hidden proceeds of an ancient crime and looted from the legionary headquarters at York. A medallion attached to the arm read – 'To the victory of the Sixth Legion, Victrix Valerius Rufus willingly and deservedly fulfilled his vow'. The Sixth Legion was a cavalry unit made up largely of Hungarian Sarmations who served on the western edges of the Roman Empire until the end of the occupation.

The air may be rich with birdsong; skylarks, curlew, grouse and even the rare 'Pennine Sparrow', or twite, make a home here. Looking back, extensive views across the Manchester Basin to the hills of mid-Cheshire and along the vale of the Mersey to distant Liverpool open out. Simply remain with this track; at the next gate keep ahead along the Pennine Bridleway for Piethorne Reservoir. A sharp valley here unveils views beyond the spectacular Rakewood Viaduct of the M62 to Hollingworth Lake, the jumble of moorland tops above Littleborough and along the line of the West Pennines. The track continues to climb past the tumbled field-walls dividing long-abandoned upland pastures of this stirring moorscape, presently reaching a major junction marked by a fingerpost and isolated stone gateposts **B**.

Carry on towards Piethorne; the track crests a pass and drops to pass the edge of Old House Ground Woods (great for bluebells), then reaches an old valve house at the head of Piethorne Reservoir (created in 1878). Now begins a long,

steady climb up the track, signed as the Pennine Bridleway for Castleshaw. The transmitter mast off to the left is at Windy Hill, near which is the highest

View north from Rooden Reservoir

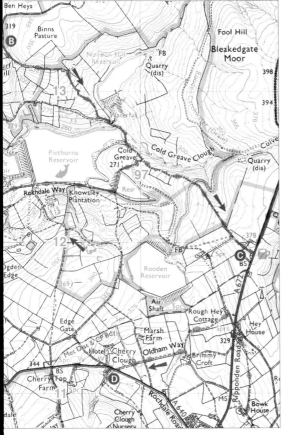

Drop through this, remaining 50 yds in-field from the wall on your right; this direction finds stiles and a flat bridge across a beck in a reedy valley. Turn left from this to a set of stiles through horse pasture beside ponds. Bear right over a wall-stile immediately beyond the stables access to find a low iron ladder-stile. Climb this and head across the reedy pastures aiming slightly left of the distant hotel. Cross a driveway via stiles, shortly reaching the main road just left of a house **D**.

Turn right; in a short distance fork right along the bridleway signed off the start of the car-parking area of the **Clough Manor Hotel**. This rough track rises past a house and continues up to a tarred drive beside Edge Gate Farm. Turn right on this, picking up a rutted, walled track. A handgate takes the track above Rooden Reservoir to find the first of a series of low stone waymark posts just beyond a ruined gateway. Keep ahead to the second post; here fork left on a narrow, level path, which trails through old quarry workings. The views from here are of remarkably remote countryside barely four miles from Rochdale town centre.

This path skims high above Piethorne Reservoir; beyond a stile a fork is reached next to an Oldham Corporation Water Works post. Bear right, putting a fence on your right. Drop to a cattle-grid and walk down to the lower road; turn left to return to the car park. ●

point on the M62 Motorway, at 1,442 ft the highest in Britain. As the track eventually levels, a magnificent view south to the distinctive peak of Shutlingsloe, deep in the Peak District, is revealed. Follow the track through a fold of houses to gain the main road beside the remarkable stone-tiled roof of the **Ram's Head Inn** at Denshaw **C**.

Turn right to walk a downhill stretch on a verge beside the main road. In 500 yds take the first turn, sharp-right, into a rough lane and immediately join the fenced grassy path here. In 75 yds (before the white cottages) turn left to a ladder-stile, cross the track and use the Oldham Way stile into rough pasture.

Ponden Kirk, Alcomden Stones & the Brontë Moors

			GPS waypoints
Start	Stanbury		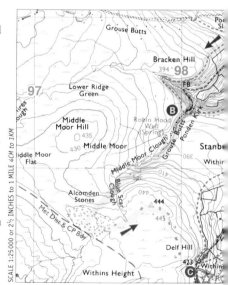 SE 012 371
Distance	6 miles (9.7km)		Ⓐ SD 995 371
Height gain	1,000 feet (305m)		Ⓑ SD 980 363
Approximate time	3½ hours		Ⓒ SD 981 353
Parking	Plenty of roadside parking at the eastern (Haworth) end of village		Ⓓ SD 997 359
Route terrain	A mixture of lanes, farm roads and paths. The last section to the Alcomden Stones involves walking unpathed heather moor which is difficult underfoot		
Dog friendly	Awkward stiles and ladder-stiles		
Ordnance Survey maps	Landrangers 103 (Blackburn & Burnley) and 104 (Leeds & Bradford), Explorer OL21 (South Pennines)		

The 'Brontë Moors' is a geographical fiction that neatly encapsulates the wild countryside west of Haworth, where Emily Brontë's tragic story Wuthering Heights *was set. From the village of Stanbury the walk heads off into Ponden Clough, passing less familiar locations featured in the novel. Rising to the exposed Alcomden Stones, marvellous views might be shared with but a handful of hardy souls before returning via the classic Top Withins and Brontë Falls.*

 Walk up through Stanbury, passing its **pubs** and school. As the road begins to descend, fork left up the 'No Through Road', signed as a footpath to Brontë Falls and 'The Heights' camping site. Walk to the junction in 400 yds; here turn right on the lane signed as a path for Buckley Green and Ponden Kirk. Pass by a farm and then keep half-right at the fold of cottages at Buckley Green, choosing the track beneath the wires. This drops to gateposts; use the handgate on the right here into a sunken path to reach the dam of Ponden Reservoir Ⓐ.

Turn left and follow the lane around the reservoir; keep right and rise to the gaggle of houses here at Ponden. On your right is Ponden Hall, a solid yeoman's farmhouse held to be the inspiration for Thrushcross Grange, family home of the Lintons in *Wuthering Heights*. Remain on the roughening lane, climbing past calf pens to a surfaced junction of tracks in 250 yds. Turn left with the fingerpost for Ponden Kirk, tracing the track up to the point it bends left into Height Laithe Farm; here keep ahead on the rougher track, over a cattle-grid and through a gate onto Walshaw and Lancashire Moor.

In 200 yds fork left at a fingerpost onto a field path for Ponden Clough, rising to another fingerpost just above the remote house. Bear right up the path beside a wall on your left. As this peels steeply down into Ponden Clough, stick with the path along the lip of the defile, gaining fine views to the clough head. Breaking the horizon on the skyline are the Alcomden Stones; nearer to hand, a distinct rocky outcrop marks the upper edge of the clough.

The path bends right into a horn of Ponden Clough, marked by lively waterfalls, before turning sharp-left along the edge of the steepening drop. As you pass the crumbling sheepfold on your right, the top of the rocky outcrop is on your left. This, Ponden Kirk, is likely to be Penistone Crag, favourite childhood haunt of Heathcliff and Cathy; the superstition-wreathed 'Fairy Cave' being the aperture at the base of the rock pillar. A short distance beyond this, the path starts to drop into the top of the gorge, reaching a path junction above a flat bridge and fingerpost **B**.

Fork right at this point, leaving the wider path to cross the footbridge while you commence a gentle climb up a thin path, the beck on your left. It is marshy underfoot in places; in a short distance cross a flat bridge and stick with the

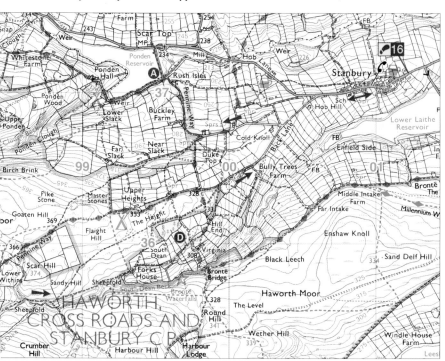

Ponden Clough from Ponden Kirk

pillar on Delf Hill. The horizons draw back to encompass Pendle Hill and the great arc of moors and hills marking the Yorkshire Dales. Head half-right from the pillar as you approached it, a good, level path through the heather and then across grassy moorland; the distant wind turbines are a confirming landmark straight ahead. The valley of Sladen Beck shortly comes into view to your left; the ruins of Top Withins **C** (perhaps the model for Wuthering Heights itself) are soon reached.

At the ruins turn left along the Pennine Way. At a fingerposted fork at the next ruin, turn right for Brontë Falls and Haworth, shallow steps dropping to become a wide, braided path, which picks up a way along the left (north) slopes of Sladen Beck. Remain with this over a ladder-stile, then through a corner gap-stile, continuing through a jigsaw of broken walls and ruins. As the path starts to drop towards a handgate, bear left on a lesser, level path to reach a fingerpost, then another just a few yards farther on, this one above a couple of trees. *If you wish to visit the nearby Brontë Falls and Bridge, turn right into the valley and then return to this point.*

Otherwise; turn half-left on the path signed for Brontë Way and Stanbury **D**. Climb a ladder-stile and cross the waist of the rough pasture, enjoying the views down to Lower Laithe Reservoir and the ridge-top village of Stanbury. Another ladder-stile leads to a path to a nearby rough lane. Turn right for Stanbury and follow this track, which presently becomes tarred, all the way through to Stanbury, keeping right at any junctions. ●

path now on the left of Middle Moor Clough. A long string of grouse butts and baffles is your companion as the clough shallows and the high moors beckon. A steep side-clough is tackled before the line of butts finally fails; your target is the area of boulders and stones about 400 yds ahead. There is no walked path through the heather; take your time to choose a route by line of sight to the rocks and rise to the upper level here. Remember this approach, as you need to turn left as you gain the top at the Alcomden Stones.

This is a truly remote place, at the edge of the largest tract of open moorland in the South Pennines. The tip of the reservoir you may glimpse is at Widdop; the wave-crest of a hill way to your right as you reach the stones is Boulsworth Hill. Curlew, oystercatcher and wheatear are your likely companions, as this is a little-visited and wild location.

Turn left along the thin path, which develops into a decent trod as it gradually bends left to the triangulation

Delph, Castleshaw & Harrop Edge

		GPS waypoints
Start	Uppermill	✎ SD 995 065
Distance	7 miles (11.3km)	**A** SD 987 074
Height gain	1,095 feet (335m)	**B** SD 982 090
Approximate time	3½ hours	**C** SD 989 102
Parking	Wool Road British Waterways public car park, ½ mile north of village centre off A670	**D** SD 998 090 **E** SD 994 074 **F** SD 992 066
Route terrain	Mostly on old railway and farm tracks, with a little road walking and some field paths	
Dog friendly	Stiles and gates need agile dogs; on leads in lambing country	
Ordnance Survey maps	Landranger 109 (Manchester), Explorers OL1 (Peak District [Dark Peak]) and OL21 (South Pennines)	

Saddleworth is an enchanting mix of gritstone mill villages, moorland, ridges, gorges and endless views. This airy walk strings through the heart of this nebulous, hilly area, passing a Roman fortlet before reaching pretty Dobcross, where Hollywood once called.

✎ Put the Huddersfield Narrow Canal – England's highest and completed in 1811 – on your right, shortly passing the Brownhill Visitor Centre, nestled between old bridges and the graceful Uppermill Viaduct, carrying the Manchester to Leeds railway high above the trough cut by the River Tame. Turn right (signed for Delph via Delph Donkey) over the footbridge just below the very deep Limekiln Lock, walk ahead to the tarred lane and fork right. Just past the skewed bridge join the trackbed of the old railway on your right. Constructed in 1851, this branch line to Delph was originally worked by a white horse pulling a single carriage and soon gained the nickname the 'Delph

Donkey'. This lovely greenway contours high above the river for well over a mile to reach the fenced boundary of a ruinous mill complex. Leave the trackbed, join the nearby main road (take care here), cross it and turn left to reach the crossroads at Delph **A**.

Dog-leg right-then-left across the main A62 and join the road ('The Sound') into Delph village. In 400 yds turn right into the public car park opposite the impressive Cooperative Hall. At the foot of the car park turn left (do not cross the footbridge) on a path between a mill-leat and the River Tame, passing an old water mill to reach the village centre. Turn right over the bridge to reach the **White Lion** pub; here turn left. In about 150 yds, turn right on Lodge Lane. At the three-way split, join the 'No Through Road' for Delph Greave Farm. Pass left of the farmhouse, following 'Horseshoe Trail' waymark discs on a grassy wall-side climb through a series of pastures and gates to reach the sturdy Georgian chapel at Heights **B**.

Turn right, passing between the churchyard and the friendly little **Royal Oak** pub (opening restricted), remaining on this, Broad Lane, as it rises gently and then deteriorates to a rough track beyond a final, renovated farmhouse on these windy heights. This is a magnificent stretch of the walk, with great views across these typical South Pennine uplands, laced by old walls and dotted with a few white-painted farmhouses amid stirring scenery.

In about one mile there is a major crossing of tracks and paths **C**; here turn right along the walled Low Gate Lane (Pennine Bridleway) and drop steeply to a T-junction and gates. Turn left to reach the dam of Castleshaw Upper Reservoir; cross this to reach Dirty Lane and turn right along this peaceful tarred road. The higher ground immediately on your left is the site of

Rigodumum Fort, built for the Roman General, Agricola in the 1st century; permissive paths (bear left at the junction just passed, then right) allow access to visit the grassy remains – the (largely wooden) fort itself was only in use for about 40 years. Stay on the lane past the lower reservoir to a sharp-right bend where the road name changes to Waterworks Lane. At this corner go ahead up the narrow track and climb the stile right of a gate. Rise with this rough path, presently gaining a tarred driveway; just before this ends turn sharp-left on a grassy path up to the main road **D**.

Join the walled track opposite and climb this to a cross-lane. Turn right here along Harrop Edge Lane. A mile's walk on this straight, rough lane brings you to the first house, Lark Hill Farm **E**. Immediately past this, turn left on the track; at the junction in 250 yds bend right on the walled way and follow it, Long Lane, ahead to the edge of Dobcross. Keep right at the end along Sandy Lane, dropping to the nearby, picturesque village centre 'Square' beside the terrific **Swan Inn**. Film fans will recognise this area as a major location used in John Schlesinger's atmospheric 1979 film *Yanks*; the little square and fabulous weaver's housing here is an exquisite example of an archetypical South Pennine weaving hamlet.

F Turn left at **The Swan Inn** along Sugar Lane. At the bend in 200 yds fork right down Nicker Brow, picking up the path beyond

The old watermill at Delph

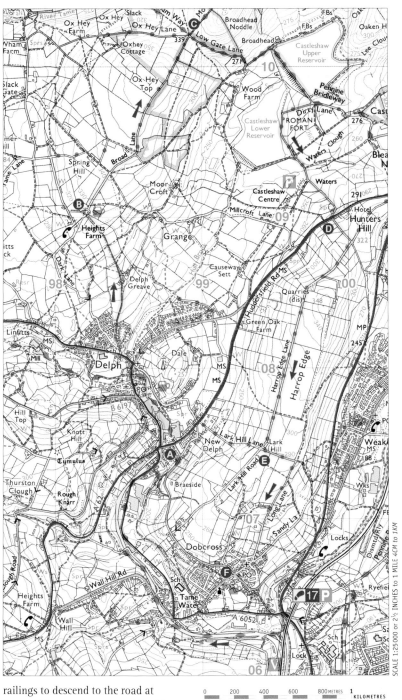

railings to descend to the road at
Brownhills near the memorable old
Bridge Mill of 1772, one of the area's
oldest. Cross the bridge, swing right and
right again through the Brownhill
complex and put the canal on your left
to return to Wool Road Car Park. ●

SCALE 1:25000 or 2½ INCHES to 1 MILE 4CM to 1KM

| 0 | 200 | 400 | 600 | 800 METRES | 1 |
| 0 | 200 | 400 | 600 YARDS | ½ | |

KILOMETRES
MILES

Steeton Moor & Newsholme Dean

		GPS waypoints
Start	Keighley (Redcar) Tarn, Steeton Moorside	
Distance	7¼ miles (11.7km)	
Height gain	1,145 feet (350m)	
Approximate time	3½ hours	
Parking	At the Tarn car park	
Route terrain	Can be awkward underfoot and potentially marshy in places between **A** & **C**, otherwise firm going on lanes and tracks. One short, very steep climb	
Dog friendly	Frequent stiles would be very difficult for dogs	
Ordnance Survey maps	Landranger 104 (Leeds & Bradford), Explorer OL21 (South Pennines)	

GPS waypoints

- ✐ SE 038 422
- **A** SE 029 435
- **B** SE 011 427
- **C** SE 009 418
- **D** SE 008 411
- **E** SE 027 405
- **F** SE 031 410

Starting from a peaceful tarn, this walk traces lanes, by-roads and paths across Steeton Moor, high above Keighley before dropping into the secluded wooded valley of Newsholme Dean. It is a delightfully varied ramble, including rich haymeadows, open moorland with grand views and well-off-the-beaten-track old weaver's hamlets.

✐ Walk along the road with the tarn on your right and remain on this lane for just over a mile; there's no footpath but the sight lines are generally good (take care on several sharp corners) and the traffic mostly light. You're already high enough to allow commanding views across the Aire Gap (where rail, road and canal all follow a trench cut through the hills cut by the River Aire) to a horizon that includes Rombalds Moor, the line of the Yorkshire Dales and many a knoll in between. Closer to hand are rich old haymeadows, separated by a filigree of stone walls. The road descends steeply to reach a side lane, just past a covered reservoir on your left **A**.

Turn left on Intake Lane and walk this to its end, at the end of a long walled straight where a cattle-grid guards the drive up to Summer House Farm. Slip through the field gate to the right here and walk slightly right, aiming to use the wall-gap halfway down the wall opposite. From here keep ahead to the strip of trees, passing through this via handgates and then walk across the rich haymeadow to a stone stile well left of the transmitters. Beyond this continue towards the distant farm, joining a walled track that strikes through to the yard here.

Pass immediately right of Valley Farm, using a gate into horse pasture. Stick by the wall on your right; in 20 paces use the thin stone stile on your right and turn left alongside the wall, walking this reedy rough pasture past the stand of stunted trees to the point below where the wall turns left. From here look ahead to the down-wall, note where it crimps downwards and aim for a point 20 yds right of this, where a stone stile crosses a low section of the wall. Go ahead across the sloping field, passing just below an area of boulders and a small old shelter. Off to your right are the distant monuments on Earl Crag. Use a field gate and walk, with a wall on your right, to the farm ahead. Slip

left, through the farmyard and along the drive to a lane **B**.

Cross into the yard at Knowl Top Farm, pass right of the house and follow the tarred driveway all the way through to the higher farmhouse. Pass immediately right of this, bend left into the yard amid barns and look for the waymark pointing right in front of a barn, which takes you through two difficult yard gates and across a slab bridge into an uneven narrow pasture, a

beck on your left. Stay close to the wall on the right of this marshy land; there's a waymarked stile that is easy to miss just above a very boggy spot where a rail fence comes in from the right.

Climb this stile and turn left up the field edge to where the fence turns away left; from here head right, aiming for a small fingerpost near the top-right corner of this wildflower-rich sloping field. Climb the stile and walk up the right-field edge to High Pole Farm. An inconspicuous little handgate gives access to the concreted yard here; walk past the house to reach a lane **⊙**.

Turn left up the lane and walk it for about 500 yds to a crest. On the right here, a waymarked bridlegate gives onto a grassy track into moorland pasture, with views ahead to the sombre moors above Oakworth and Haworth. Keep faith with the fence/wall on your left for around 700 yds to reach, on your left, another bridlegate into a thin, walled, grassy strip, at the far end of which a lane is met **⊙**.

Turn left along this, Greystones Lane, immediately benefiting from a view into the deep, wooded chasm of Newsholme Dean. Ignore the first waymarked track sharply back-right, which heads for a farm, but do join the next track on the

Haymeadow above Summer House

right just 50 paces later, a bridlepath sign marking the route which shortly uses a gate before developing as a partly paved old track down into the Dean. Remain with this, which roughens considerably as it angles down the hillside to merge with a dirt field road. Keep left along this, round the bend and through a couple of gates to reach (100 yds beyond a summerhouse) a cottage at Newsholme Dean.

Turn left up the gravely track for 10 paces and then fork right with the waymarked footpath in front of the house; this becomes a walled old way above Dean Beck. At a split keep left, ignoring the footbridge down on the right; the path continues above the beck, presently passing above a millpond, which has enormous goldfish. Stay with the path across a footbridge and along a lovely wooded way to reach a lane **⊙**. Turn left to Goose Eye.

The building on your left is an old mill converted into housing; at the heart of this secluded hamlet is another large old mill – now apartments and, on your left, the splendid **Turkey Inn**. A fearsomely steep lane takes you out of the settlement; at the sharp-left bend slip right along the narrow, walled ginnel, rising steeply to a fold of multi-storey cottages at the lovely hillside village of Laycock. Walk ahead past old cottages and barns to reach a graveyard on your left; turn left here up Chapel Lane. At the sharp bend in 100 yds, turn right along a rougher track **⊙**, which strikes past further cottages and housing to end at gates into sloping pastures. Head slightly left on a path rising to and through a line of easily visible gap-stiles. At the small barns, use the handgate and then a waymarked gate-side stile, cutting up a final grassy pasture to a lane. Turn right to return to the Tarn. ●

The Bridestones

		GPS waypoints
Start	Todmorden	✎ SD 927 248
Distance	7¼ miles (11.7km)	Ⓐ SD 941 251
Height gain	1,180 feet (360m)	Ⓑ SD 932 259
Approximate time	3½ hours	Ⓒ SD 932 267
Parking	Ewood Lane (Sports Centre) public car park, rear of Centre Vale Park, ½ mile northwest of town centre off A646	Ⓓ SD 914 275
		Ⓔ SD 921 266
Route terrain	Pavements, farm roads, lanes and moorland paths	
Ordnance Survey maps	Landranger 103 (Blackburn & Burnley), Explorer OL21 (South Pennines)	

The sturdy old textile town of Todmorden stands in the Calder Gorge amid stunning crags, cliffs, hanging woodlands and ravine-like side valleys plunging down from the high moors. This undulating route climbs steeply to an eerie landscape of crags and pinnacles, many weathered into fantastical shapes by millennia of wind and rain, the most notable being The Bridestones, returning past pleasant woodlands and beside the infant River Calder.

✎ Find the bowling greens below the car park and walk to the diagonally opposite (far left) corner of the huge Centre Vale Park. Use the nearby pedestrian crossing and turn right towards Todmorden centre. In 100 yds, turn left into Victoria Road and follow this to and beneath the railway bridge. Fork left at **The Fountain Inn**, commencing a long, steady climb up Meadow Bottom Road; this becomes Hole Bottom Road, simply keep uphill past rows of solid terraced houses to the point where this ends at a fork. Here, bear right into the yard, walking the rough lane through this fold of old stone cottages and beyond up a steepening track. This swings left, presently reaching the edge of a small lodge (millpond). Turn left and continue uphill towards the rocky outcrop visible ahead.

At the cross-path next to the corner of a golf course Ⓐ, turn left along an old walled path that passes well below the rocks. The height already gained is rewarded with some sublime views across Todmorden to the enclosing moorlands to the south and west and also up the great cleft leading to the Cliviger Gorge, a long series of spectacular crags formed at the end of the last Ice Age that start just outside Todmorden's town centre and stretch to the watershed with the Lancashire Calder at Fair Hill summit, halfway to Burnley.

The path meanders above attractive woodland before dropping to a crossing of tracks near a terrace of stone cottages. Here turn right and walk up

The Bridestones

the rough lane past these cottages and then a single cottage before bending left and rising steeply beside a wall, in time reaching a farm. Walk into the farmyard and turn left between the small breezeblock stores. Trace this track past a large barn (right) and then ahead through a gate and along a walled greenway. Gaining rough pasture, head slightly left, guided by low posts which direct you to a rough lane; turn right a few paces along this and then keep ahead off the sharp bend. Use the bridlegate and meander along this easy path above the farm; beyond a second bridlegate the track becomes a long-established way along worn causey-stones, skirting the flank of Whirlaw Rocks and rising very easily to a metal gate **B**.

Turn right on the rising path that charts a course left of Whirlaw Rocks themselves – it's an easy scramble (and slight diversion) up to the summit boulders and the great views which include the monument on distant Stoodley Pike. The path enters a walled-track phase to reach the end of a tarred lane (note the Easter Island-style carved stone here). Turn left and walk this to its end; here turn left along the wider road.

At the end of the wall on your left, slip through the hand-gate and walk the distinct path across the reedy moorland to reach the start of the Bridestones crags. Of immediate note is the lollipop-like stone, now almost terminally undercut but still defying gravity. Locals and rock climbers have given distinct rocks individual names; hence we have the Indian's Head, The Cheese-block, Little Brother and Big Sister as well as the spectacular pinnacle rock of Bridestone herself and the fallen 'Groom' nearby. The rocks themselves are, morphologically, gritstone tors formed by a combination of subsurface weathering, freeze-thaw during periglacial times 13,000 years ago and ongoing erosion by wind and rain.

C A path strings a way along the line of crags for over ½ mile, roughly following the southern band of rocks. Eventually a wide moorland track develops; this drops to a gate-side stile, climb this and turn right to the road. The way is left – **The Sportsman's Inn** is 150 yds to your right here – along this fairly quiet road for a mile. Up to your right, more shapely outcrops draw the eye before, at a sharp-right bend, you turn left along the lane for Shore and Todmorden **D**. Descend the lane for 350 yds before turning left on a rough track, signed as a bridleway, just past a house on your right. Over the wall to your left is the Mount Cross, a pre-Norman wayside cross on an ancient route across the moors, possibly a waymark on a pilgrimage route.

Remain on this track, walking immediately left of Lower Intake Farm to reach a cross-track; turn right for Blue Bell Lane. At Coppy Stone Barn turn left on the gravelled track to reach the memorable old farmhouse at Hartley Royd. Turn left on the bridleway; go

through the gate and fork right along
the grassy track, shortly crossing
Hudson Bridge **E**.

Turn right off this and join a muddy
path around a shoulder of moorland,
coursing high above the deep clough on
your right. At a corner gate keep left,
above the wall and below Orchan
Rocks, the final crag on this walk. The
path reaches a stile into a rough track;
cross straight over and use the squeeze-
stile into a horse pasture. At the next

corner use the tiny handgate and drop
beside the barn (left) to gain an access
lane. Go ahead on this a few paces
before using another tiny gate on the
left; now walk the field-edge path
ahead to the next corner and slip
through a further gate here. Drop to the
bridge over the culvert and then ahead
a few paces, to a rough lane. Turn right
and remain with this tranquil track all
the way down to the main valley road.
Turn left, cross the road and walk beside
the little River Calder to the bridge,
right, into Ewood Lane and the road to
the car park. ●

Ripponden &
the Ryburn Valley

		GPS waypoints
Start	Booth Wood Reservoir, south of Ripponden on the A672	👣 SE 031 165
Distance	6¼ miles (10km)	Ⓐ SE 038 178
Height gain	1,280 feet (390m)	Ⓑ SE 040 191
Approximate time	3½ hours	Ⓒ SE 040 197
Parking	Public car park at Booth Wood Reservoir	Ⓓ SE 035 188 Ⓔ SE 024 187
Route terrain	Mostly good lanes and tracks, some wet moorland	Ⓕ SE 017 180
Dog friendly	Several difficult step-stiles and ladder-stiles to cross	
Ordnance Survey maps	Landrangers 109 (Manchester) & 110 (Sheffield & Huddersfield), Explorer OL21 (South Pennines)	

From a reservoir well-known to drivers on the M62, this walk meanders along lanes to the striking old mill village of Ripponden, before tracing woodland tracks up the tranquil Ryburn Valley to a secluded reservoir. From here, rising ways climb onto Blackwood Edge, revealing a grand panorama of moors and milltowns typical of the South Pennines.

👣 The fingerpost at the foot of the car park points the way down a steep, grassy path to a tarred track. Turn left on this to the nearby lane and turn right down this. Ahead is the precipitous concrete wall of the Booth Wood Dam; the lane curls below this and starts a gentle rise up the southern flank of Booth Dean Clough. To the right, the roar of the nearby M62 is diverting, but soon enough the lane, little more than an eroded tarred track, bends away from England's highest motorway and the noise subsides. At the fork below Smithy Fold Farm keep left on Smithy Lane; the road threads past cottages and farmsteads, keep ahead against a fork and downhill round a sharp-right bend to reach a short, cobbled section beside Spread Eagle House Ⓐ.

Fork right off the sharp bend here, picking up an old packhorse track which drops to cross a tiny iron footbridge and turns sharp left, rising gradually as a walled, occasionally setted (cobbled) way above the straggling village of Rishworth, centred around its bold old mill and tiny church nestled amid trees in the steep pastures below Pike End hill. This valleyside track, Heys Lane, offers ever-better views ahead into the Ryburn Valley and west to the enfolding moors. Keep ahead as the track becomes tarred, remaining with it to the far end of the little beech wood that climbs the hillside on your right Ⓑ.

Turn left with the bridleway sign for Quaker Lane on a tarred side-road; in a further 20 paces turn right at a footpath fingerpost for Ripponden Village, walking beside the wall to the fold of cottages here. Bend left and then turn right past the lower cottage, using two gap-stiles to access a superb example of an old causey path, a walled footpath floored by stone blocks, originally created maybe 300 years ago. *Take care – the stones can be very slippery in wet weather.* Remain on this to cross the old railway bridge (the line lost its passenger services in summer 1929) and turn right down the embowered path to reach a road. Cross over, drop down a couple of steps and walk through the parking area to a lane. Turn left to reach St Bartholomew's Church at the heart of old Ripponden and walk ahead to reach the old cobbled packhorse bridge across

The old village centre at Ripponden

the River Ryburn **C**.

The way is ahead-left into the yard of cottages at Mill Fold, but first take the time to cross the bridge to visit Yorkshire's oldest pub, **The Old Bridge Inn**, which dates from 1307. In Mill Fold, pass under the arched bridge and go ahead on the rough lane between industrial buildings to reach a park. Walk straight through; at the far end, just behind the basketball hoop, slip through the gate and bear right on a tarred lane, remaining on this past further units, walking an increasingly peaceful track above the river beside meadows. As the tarred lane enters private land, bear right on the earth path, remaining on this above shoots and rapids to reach a footbridge below secluded cottages. Do not cross this; instead climb the steps on your left and turn right, rising gently through the woods. At the corner junction keep right, continuing on the rougher causey path to more steps up to a bridge. Turn right to the main road **D**.

Turn right and cross the road. At the corner turn left at the bus shelter into Bar Lane. Remain with this old lane past a string of cottages and millponds, in ½ mile climbing on a cobbled track above new houses to reach a hairpin bend. Keep left here, on a thin, waymarked path left of the garage, which shortly climbs stone steps to the dam empounding Ryburn Reservoir **E**. Cross the dam and turn right along the wide path at the far side. Follow this to the narrow head of the lake; here go ahead on a rising path for Long Causeway, shortly keeping left at a split and along the walled/fenced path out of the bluebell woods. This bends left; at a T-junction turn right to reach a road **F**.

Turn left up the road to reach a farm drive on the right in 275 yds; walk along this to reach Blackwood Farm. At the farmhouse, turn left and climb the waymarked steps into a sloping pasture; at the head of this, use a hand-gate and continue up the steepening hillside by the wall on your left. Ignore the ladder-stile on your left and keep ahead to crest the ridge. A more remote, desolate view than that to the right is difficult to imagine; reedy, windswept acres undulating up to Dog Hill and Rishworth Moor. In contrast, a very busy view stretches east across Kirklees and the old woollen towns.

The path peels away from the wall to reach a stone step-stile about 70 yds up from the corner. Climb this and walk to the right of the farmhouse; cross the old track, use the ladder-stile and then walk down the rough drive. Ahead, the M62 slices across the flank of the long ridge of Moss Moor Edge; here is the famous Stott Hall Farm, isolated between the motorway carriageways. The track swings left to pass behind the imposing Rishworth Lodge, presently reaching a tarred lane at a T-junction beyond a spinney. Turn right, then in 50 paces sharp left on a rough lane which leads to and through a fold of cottages. Remain on the lane to reach the main road opposite the car park. ●

Heber's Ghyll & Rombalds Moor

		GPS waypoints
Start	Ilkley: Heber's Ghyll Drive, western edge of town, off Grove Road	✔ SE 100 473
Distance	8½ miles (13.7km)	Ⓐ SE 085 470
		Ⓑ SE 092 456
Height gain	1,115 feet (340m)	Ⓒ SE 120 448
Approximate time	4 hours	Ⓓ SE 130 462
Parking	Small lay-by (or roadside) on the left, as the woods start	Ⓔ SE 130 466
		Ⓕ SE 117 467
Route terrain	One steep climb to start. Moorland paths and tracks, boggy in places. One short stretch of rough, un-pathed heather moor	
Ordnance Survey maps	Landranger 104 (Leeds & Bradford), Explorer 297 (Lower Wharfedale & Washburn Valley)	

Rombalds, the high moorland bloc between the valleys of the Rivers Aire and Wharfe, is fragmented into countless subdivisions, the most famous of which is Ilkley Moor, the subject of the renowned 'Yorkshire National Anthem'. This energetic walk encounters a grand selection of the moor's treasures, both man-made and natural, accompanied by sublime views to the nearby Yorkshire Dales and along the Pennines. The deceptively steep start is up the beautiful, secluded Heber's Clough. It should not be attempted in foggy or snowy conditions unless you are well experienced in such and carry the appropriate equipment.

✎ Take the right-hand path for Heber's Ghyll, cross a footbridge and pass left of the stone building. A steep climb up this exquisite wooded clough, crossing and re-crossing Black Beck, eventually reaches a walled-seat; turn left with the fingerpost to a metal kissing-gate out of the woods. Go straight over the main path (not over the bridge), up a path directly behind the fingerpost to gain a wider cross-path.

Turn right, soon joining a compacted path along the lip of the natural moorland step, giving excellent views up the Wharfe Valley before reaching the railed enclosure protecting the carved 'Swastika Stone'. The easily visible one is a Victorian copy of the original, weathered one on the same slab. It may date from the Bronze Age; experts identify its alignment with the equinoctial sunrise. Remain with the wide path over stone step-stiles and then two metal hand-gates beyond a stand of low, spreading pines.

Beyond the second gate Ⓐ, turn left

parallel to the wall. There's no obvious path through the undergrowth, the going eases after 50 yds. Where the wall turns left, head half-left on a reedy path; in 100 yds turn half-right on a thin path straight up the steep hillside, following a shallow cleft to level out on a plateau. Continue ahead to the gap in the distant line of conifers; here turn left on the part-paved track outside the wall. This, marshy in places, rises to a corner just outside the woods at craggy outcrops, the East and West Buck Stones **B** at the heart of Rombalds Moor, Rombald being a mythological giant who lived on these inhospitable heights.

Turn left, putting the wall on your right. Way off to your left, the horizon is stippled by the puffball-like radomes of Menwith Hill Early Warning Radar Station; to your right, distant moorland edges rise above the Aire and Calder Valleys. Continue past the masts at Whetstone Gate; a further mile reaches a point where the wall kinks to the right at a field-gate and hand-gate at White Crag **C**.

Use neither gate; instead take the faint moorland road heading away from this corner at 10 o'clock as you approached it. This track passes a boundary stone, followed by a yellow-topped post to reach a wide cross-path and another stone known as Lanshaw Lad. Turn right to visit the nearby Twelve Apostles Stone Circle, an evocative site that once had far more stones. Return towards Lanshaw Lad, but turn right just before it along the Millennium Way Circular Walk. The path crosses a long stretch of boardwalk, at the far end of which turn right on a lesser path. In 20 paces fork left on a grassier way, which undulates across the damp moor, gradually bending right above a shallow clough on your left. At a fork keep right on the higher option, which shortly starts to lose height; you're walking directly towards the transmitter mast on distant Norwood Edge. Beyond a boggy area the path shortly reaches a main cross path **D**.

Turn left to the isolated stone block, Haystack Rock, said to resemble an olden-day haystack. Look for the Cup & Ring marks carved into the shallower-angled eastern face. These at Haystack are clearly visible, but the purpose of the Bronze Age petroglyphs is

ILKLEY

Sch · Hosp · Sch

Hotel · 148 · Ben Rhydding

norama Rocks · FB · 152 · FB

Intake Heads · Reservoir · Millennium Way · Cup & Ring-marked Rock · Resr

Barmishaw · Ford · White Wells · Cow and Calf

er Well ottage · FB · Cup & Ring-marked Rock · West Rock · Rocky Valley · Quarries (disused) · Hotel

Cup & Ring-marked Rocks · Quarries (disused) · Cup-marked Rock · Ilkley Crags · Cup & Ring-marked Rocks

Rock · Cup & Ring-marked Rocks · Wicken Tree Crag · Cranshaw Thorn Hill · Reservoir

Grainings Head · Cup-marked Rock · Ilkley Moor · Cup & Ring marked Rocks · Pancake Stone · Cup-marked Rock

Waterfall · Badger Stone · Cup-marked Rock · Enclosure

Cup & Ring-marked Rock · Gill Head · Cup & Ring-marked Rocks

Green Gates · Green Crag

Grouse Butts · Dales Way Link · Lanshaw Delves

hetstone Gate · Grouse Butts · Lanshaw

Wireless Station · White Crag Moss · Lanshaw

Thimble Stones · BS · Cairn · 402 · Lanshaw Lad (BS) · Twelve Apostles Stone Circle · High Lanshaw Dam

45 · BS · White Crag

The Two Eggs · White Crag · Ashlar Chair

High Moor · 368

Moor

SCALE 1:25000 or 2½ INCHES to 1 MILE 4CM to 1KM

0 200 400 600 800 METRES 1 KILOMETRES
0 200 400 600 YARDS ½ MILES

unknown. Head away from the carved face on a narrow path which drops to the nearby craggy outcrop; from here walk to the distinctive crag of Cow and Calf Rocks. The Cow is the main crag; the Calf the large, fallen boulder below. Aim to keep to the high ground immediately left of the Cow **E**.

There's a small old quarry here; turn left from the grassy area just this side of it on a wide, braided path (pines off to your right) which heads for the cliffs of Ilkley Crag. Cross Blackstone Beck Falls near the top of a clough, shortly reaching the top of the aptly named Rocky Valley. Walk down this; as the sides peel back there are great views across Ilkley and up Wharfedale. The path undulates

below steep crags to reach a white-painted cottage, White Wells **F**. This was one of the original baths at the start of the development of Ilkley as a popular hydropathic health spa; the cold baths here opened in about 1780, past users included Charles Darwin.

Fork left at White Wells on the wide gravely path. Just after crossing a cobbled area at a sharp-right bend above a fall of water, turn left on a lesser, level, compacted stone path, and remain with this, presently crossing directly over a tarred lane. Stay on the gently rising path beside walled gardens, eventually passing above the little Panorama Reservoir. Cross the footbridge just beyond this and then make use of the kissing-gate on the right, dropping with the path back down Heber's Ghyll. ●

Luddenden Dean, Midgley Moor & Churn Milk Joan

		GPS waypoints
Start	Jerusalem Farm Nature Reserve, Luddenden Dean	⬛ SE 036 278
Distance	8½ miles (13.7km)	Ⓐ SE 035 286
		Ⓑ SE 027 293
Height gain	1,065 feet (325m)	Ⓒ SE 029 314
Approximate time	4 hours	Ⓓ SE 013 300
		Ⓔ SE 017 290
Parking	Jerusalem Farm Nature Reserve	Ⓕ SE 020 276
Route terrain	Steep climb to start, then lanes and farm tracks, with a long section of moorland walking	Ⓖ SE 034 274
Dog friendly	Dogs strictly on leads between February and July on Access Land	
Ordnance Survey maps	Landranger 104 (Leeds & Bradford), Explorer OL21 (South Pennines)	

The dimpled moors to the west of Halifax tumble into a cauldron holding a glorious mosaic of pastures and pocket woodlands and hamlets collectively known as Luddenden Dean, a serene, green fold in the hills. From the Dean, paths and lanes climb steadily to moorland edge tracks; the walk then traces a series of catchwater drains on a magnificent circuit of these high moors before reaching Churn Milk Joan, an enigmatic stone pillar steeped in legend.

⬛ Use the 'V' stile at the bottom of the car park and cross the bridge over Luddenden Brook. Head slightly right (2 o'clock) up the timber-edged path rising to the right of the rocky slab. In 150 yds turn sharp left, continuing to rise through the woods. Ignore a sign to the right for Saltonstall; here keep ahead, soon joining a path beside a wall with haymeadows to your left. This develops as a walled track, rising to a secluded house; turn right up the grassed garden and then the driveway to reach a junction. Turn right to the nearby junction; here turn left up the

bridleway, pass a farm and continue up to a rough lane Ⓐ.

Bear left, passing Upper Green Edge Farm; keep ahead-right at the first junction and then ahead-left along the tarred lane to reach an arched building across the lane. Castle Carr House was a vast castellated mansion built in 1859 for Captain Joseph Priestley Edwards but inhabited for barely 20 years; Edwards himself died in an accident before it was completed. Becoming

0	200	400	600	800 METRES	1	
						KILOMETRES
						MILES
0	200	400	600 YARDS		½	

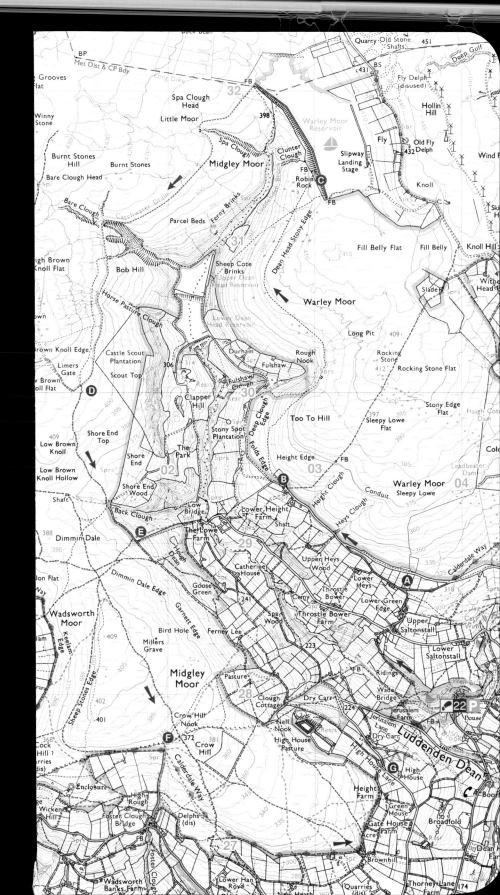

dilapidated, it was demolished in the 1960s leaving the Gothic gatehouse as a tantalising reminder of former grandeur.

Take the path to the right just before the gatehouse **B**; a stile at the top of steps issues into a clear path up the reedy pasture, gradually bending left to an old stile and, beyond, a footbridge over a derelict catchwater drain. Turn left along this old watercourse (easiest on its left) and remain with it for the next mile. In places it disappears from view, but the path is obvious. Down to your left, the ruins of Castle Carr House nestle amid a forest of rhododendrons below Dean Head Reservoirs. This moorland of Warley Moor has a healthy population of upland birds; golden plover, twite, curlew and grouse thrive here. The path eventually merges with a shooters road; keep ahead to a valve-house **C** at the foot of the dam at Fly Flatts (Warley Moor) Reservoir.

Bear left up the grassy dam to gain the reservoir-edge path; turn left along this and walk to the near corner of the reservoir. Turn left beside a deep concrete catchwater drain; remain with this for the next 1½ miles to reach a point where a walled corner is just off to your left. In another 150 yds is a stone bridge across the drain and a low wooden post beside the path **D**.

Turn left here on a bridleway and trace a lesser ditch, losing a little height before reaching another walled corner. Keep ahead on a rough track beside the fence/wall on your left. In 200 yds, at the point where this turns away (and a broken wall continues ahead), a cross-path is encountered; turn right on this **E** and rise easily with it. Go straight across a thin path, shortly bearing right along a wider way that crests at a cross-track marked by a small cairn. Turn left on a wide, muddy track which bends

gradually right in 150 yds. As it gains height, fine views open out across the Calder Valley to Stoodley Pike and the sweep of moors beyond.

In a further 250 yds, take the left option at a fork *(not the fork near a grouse butt),* a narrower path through the heather and bilberry, soon losing the valley views. The giant transmitter mast on Emley Moor is your waymark as you head across an open area; then a slim standing stone calls the path directly to it. This is Churn Milk Joan **F**.

This enigmatic pillar inspired several legends; one that it marks the spot where a milkmaid died from hypothermia while carrying milk across these moors, while locally born Poet Laureate Ted Hughes winds a poem around the stone. Less prosaically, the stone probably marks the boundary between the Lordships of Midgley and Wadsworth. There's a tradition that you should leave a coin in the hollow on the stone's top, reclaiming a coin from previous walkers' offerings.

Walk in-line straight down past the stone, joining the Calderdale Way (yellow topped posts with a 'carpet-beater' symbol). The path curls left beneath the snout of Midgley Moor, revealing splendid views into Luddenden Dean. At a waymarked post at a fenced corner keep left, putting a wall/fence on your right. Pass above a farmhouse, presently joining a tarred access road via a stile **G**.

This lane swings sharply right to a junction; here go left on Dry Carr Lane. In 300 yds, at the last farmhouse, turn sharp right down the brick driveway to find a waymarked hand-gate to the building's right. The grassy path falls beside a wall to a hand-gate beneath an oak tree; slip through this and drop to a lane beside a barn. Turn right to return to the start. ●

Cowpe Moss &
the Famine Road

		GPS waypoints	
Start	Cowpe, picnic site at Cowpe village	🔖	SD 834 214
Distance	7½ miles (12km)	Ⓐ	SD 828 209
Height gain	1,210 feet (370m)	Ⓑ	SD 818 212
Approximate time	4 hours	Ⓒ	SD 821 205
Parking	Follow 'Picnic Site' signs up Cowpe	Ⓓ	SD 827 203
	Road from mini-roundabout on	Ⓔ	SD 832 187
	A681 in Waterfoot [c.½ mile]	Ⓕ	SD 857 184
		Ⓖ	SD 850 196
Route terrain	Old quarry roads and tracks, some short paths through tussocky moorland grasses		
Dog friendly	A few awkward stiles		
Ordnance Survey maps	Landranger 103 (Blackburn & Burnley), Explorer OL21 (South Pennines)		

The hills above the Irwell Valley were turned inside out by Victorian quarrymen in their search for sandstone slab to pave the thoroughfares of the Industrial Revolution's burgeoning towns and cities. The landscape is slightly melancholic, but offers an absorbing diversion amid the windy moors. Today this wind is harvested by huge turbines, the shadows of which pass silently across the remains of tramroads and cartways, re-born as the Pennine Bridleway.

🔖 Leave the picnic site entrance and go ahead 50 yds (not immediately right) to the tarred lane. Here fork right to commence a long, steady climb out of the valley of Cowpe Brook. The lane ends among renovated farmsteads; pass between the houses and bend left up a fenced track, continuing beyond a stile on a rough field track, rising to reach tumbled ruins Ⓐ. The hard work is largely over. Take the stile on your right, gaining the line of a fragmented track around the flank of Cowpe Lowe hill. From the well-wooded valley below, the old mill towns of the upper Irwell Valley – Rawtenstall, Waterfoot and Bacup –

reach towards the encircling moors. Beyond these, insubstantial horizons feature the Forest of Bowland, Pendle Hill and Pen-y-Ghent. Persevere along this braided way (occasionally waymarked) for 800 yds, presently rising very gently to find a redundant walled corner marked with RW (Rossendale Way) and Access Land discs; from here walk to the obvious, tall gateposts ahead-left. Pass through and turn right beside the wall to reach an old track 200 yds away Ⓑ.

Turn left; soon the first abandoned quarry workings pit the land below Cowpe Lowe here, while ahead, the turbines of the wind farm on Scout Moor feather the horizon. The part-paved track gradually bends left; off to your right, the distant ridge is capped by the Peel Monument high above Ramsbottom. The track leads to a stile and fingerpost **C** amid old walls and vaccary fencing (the upright slabs); beyond here join the upper of two closely parallel tracks, again partly paved with worn slabs. Favour the upper level, which is the line of one of the area's former tramroads; this becomes more obvious as it curves right along an embankment and past a fallen bridge to reach a Pennine Bridleway fingerpost **D**.

Face towards Top of Leach but do not walk the main track; instead fork half-right on a lesser, reedy track and walk this to and past an old stone gatepost. The track becomes more pronounced as Waugh Well Reservoir becomes visible below. Join the concreted service road for a short while before keeping left on a level path, leaving the roadway to drop away. In a short distance an information board reveals your location as below Foe Edge, a regular haunt of the Victorian writer Edwin Waugh. Waugh (1817-90) was the doyen of Lancashire's Dialect Poets. Much of his work was inspired by these uplands; what would he make of the new interlopers, the vast turbines, which labour languorously with the breeze, uttering a strange, ghostly call as they turn? Continue on the path beyond a nearby stile to reach a memorial to Waugh in a fittingly wild location.

Beyond this much-loved memorial, the path narrows and climbs an increasingly constricted clough, culminating in small waterfalls and a memorable view back across the reservoir to the distant, shadowy form of the Bowland Fells beyond Longridge

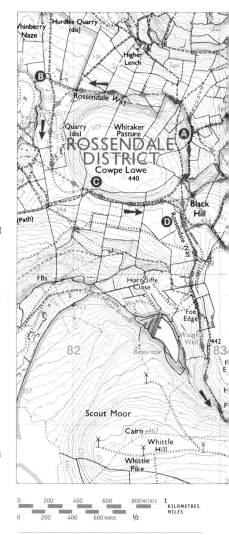

Fell's long ridge. Levelling beside a broken wall, continue this fractured way past two stone gateposts to gain the service road for the Scout Moor Wind Farm **E**. Turbines are everywhere, skirting the flat-topped Knowl Hill but only partly diverting attention from the sweeping panorama ahead that stretches across the Manchester Basin to the Peak District, Cheshire Plain and on clear days the Wrekin in Shropshire and the Clwydian Mountains in North Wales.

Turn left; then fork left at the

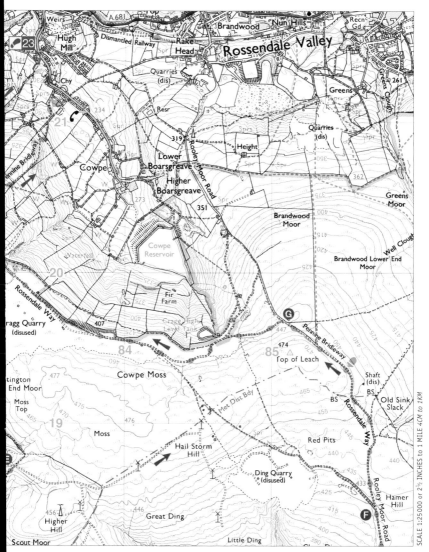

junction and walk this wide scar across the moors to reach the outermost giant windmill (NX 80648). Pass immediately left of this and leave the service road; in 150 yds, just past shallow pools you'll reach low ruins. Turn right here on a low, embanked path; this appears to have been some sort of inter-quarry trackway as it passes old loading platforms before dropping to Ding Quarry. The long-abandoned workings here are controversial, as old permissions to reopen workings vie

against fierce opposition guaranteeing a long fight before a final decision is made. You need to reach the old access track that peels away gradually to the left from the left-edge of the delvings. Once on this, remain with it to meet with a wider moorland road **F** in a further ¼ mile.

A low Pennine Bridleway post confirms your correct position here. Turn left on this highly improbable route, a cobbled highway to the stars. This monumental feat of construction is

Rooley Moor Road, an old packhorse route linking the Rossendale Valley and Rochdale. It was upgraded in the 1860s to provide unemployment relief for workers in the local textile industry, made redundant as a result of the American Civil War; the Union navy blockaded the ports of the Confederate South, cutting off supplies of the raw cotton upon which much of the Lancashire textile industry relied. It quickly became known as the 'Cotton Famine Road'; thirsty workers doubtless sought sustenance at the remote Moorcock Inn that stood on these heights until the 1920s. The cobbles eventually give way to another worn-stone cartway and reach a major fork in the track in about one mile **G**.

Turn left on the Pennine Bridleway for Waterfoot, which, beyond a gate, now passes through the 'Rossendale Alps', the sturdy spoil-tips of Cragg Quarry's massive workings. Views to

The Pennine Bridleway at Foe Edge

the northern horizon are astonishing. In the middle distance, beyond the deep-green Cowpe and Irwell Valleys, the great whaleback is Pendle Hill while much farther beyond are the distinct forms of Pen-y-Ghent and Ingleborough, two of the Yorkshire Dales' famous Three Peaks. The old industrial artery passes beyond the workings and, beyond a gate, shortly bends left. Keep right at a fork and drop down to a familiar Pennine Bridleway fingerpost **D**.

This time, fork right towards Waterfoot, commencing an easy descent off the moors along a snaking, stony, old field road, passing through several gates and waymarked here and there as the Mary Towneley Loop of the Pennine Bridleway. This way eventually delivers you onto the village road in Cowpe beside the excellent pub, **The Buck**. Turn left and wind with the road to reach Green Bridge South terrace on your right. Just beyond, on the left, is the lane to the picnic site.   ●

Crimsworth Dean, Walshaw & Hebden Dale

Start	Hardcastle Crags NT car park, Midgehole	**GPS waypoints**
Distance	8¼ miles (13.3km)	✎ SD 988 292
		Ⓐ SD 989 313
Height gain	1,310 feet (400m)	Ⓑ SD 955 321
		Ⓒ SD 951 316
Approximate time	4 hours	Ⓓ SD 957 313
Parking	Hardcastle Crags NT car park signed off Keighley Road (A6033) above Hebden Bridge	Ⓔ SD 973 309
		Ⓕ SD 973 298
Route terrain	Mostly good lanes and tracks, with some rough walking and one short, sharp climb	
Dog friendly	Several ladder-stiles en route. Dogs on leads on the upland sections in sheep country	
Ordnance Survey maps	Landranger 103 (Blackburn & Burnley), Explorer OL21 (South Pennines)	

Deep wooded gorges and sinuous cloughs feed tributaries of the Yorkshire River Calder above the fashionable town of Hebden Bridge. This walk explores the stark, haunting landscape, climbing into archetypical South Pennine hill country, to the secluded hamlet of Walshaw and a remote old drovers' pub high on the moors. The final flourish is a memorable descent through magnificent woodlands clothing Hebden Dale, below Hardcastle Crags and past secluded Gibson Mill.

✎ Walk uphill from the car park, shortly passing the NT Estate Office at Hollin Hall. Beyond here the tarred lane becomes unsurfaced, continuing a gradual climb up the flank of Crimsworth Dean, the delightful wooded valley to your right. Beyond an isolated farm the lane becomes a rough, walled track, levelling out before reaching a melancholic, ruined laithe house (farmhouse and cattle-house share the same roof) Ⓐ.

Turn left on the Pennine Bridleway 'Calder-Aire Link', rising to a gate just above another ruin. Turn left on an old moorland track beside a wall. At the next gate, swap sides of the wall and then trace this gradually downhill. Several gates bring you to the remote hamlet of Walshaw; keep ahead through this on the level lane, past New Laithes Farm to reach the valley of Alcomden Water. Cross the stone bridge and walk to the nearby ruin Ⓑ.

Take the grassy path that rises left just past the building; at the track look left for the fingerposted stile a few paces away on the right. The way rises beside a fence above a beck; at the fence corner, walk ahead from the low waymarked post for 50 paces and then drift gradually left across the low, tussocky rise. You'll see the white-painted **Pack Horse Inn** across the rough, marshy pasture; head for this and two ladder-stiles will bring you to the road here **C**. The pub has fascinating plans, maps and photos of the local reservoirs and industrial railways of a century ago.

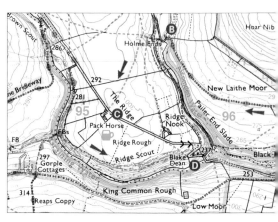

Facing the pub, turn right to use another ladder-stile on the left in 100 yds; walk beside the tumbled wall to use another stile and turn left. At the adjoining Pennine Way junction, remain on the higher level along the lip of the deep clough of Graining Water. The braided path gradually drops to meet a road at a hairpin bend **D**.

Turn downhill past the scout hut. At the bend, fork left past the barrier into a walled track. At the next bend, use the waymarked hand-gate, descend the steep steps and cross the nearby footbridge. Choose the path beside Hebden Water and walk downstream. The route presently reaches a series of stone abutments across the river, remnants of the short-lived Blakedean

Hebden Water at Black Dean

Railway, a 3ft-gauge line built in the early 1900s when the Walshaw Dean Reservoirs higher up the valley were created. The line's highlight was a 700ft-long trestle viaduct built of pitch pine; these abutments supported this viaduct, demolished in 1912.

Here you need to tackle the steep valley-side on your left; choose a sheep path and climb straight up to reach a wide, green cross-track. Turn right on this to reach a hand-gate through a fence. Pick up the good path beyond, soon heading into the woods at this upper end of Hebden Dale. The mostly level path reaches a secluded cottage at Over Wood. Join the rough access road and wind with it through these beautiful mixed woodlands of pine, oak and birch, thickly carpeted with bluebells and bright with stitchwort in spring.

In ½ mile you'll cross a flat, sheet-iron bridge over a beck **E**. Turn right on the path through a grove of beech, cross the footbridge and head downstream. For the

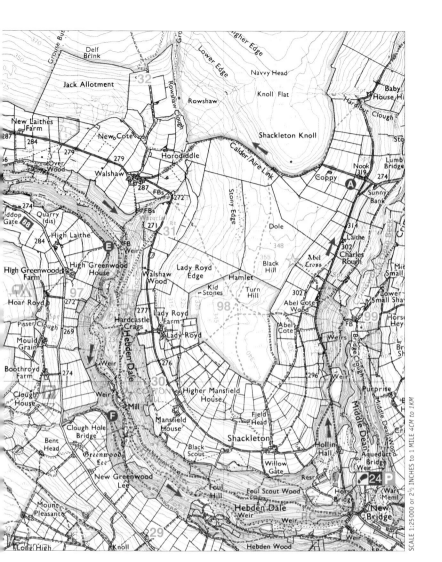

SCALE 1:25000 or 2½ INCHES to 1 MILE 4CM to 1KM

next mile the path sticks close to the river through the rocky gorge, criss-crossing on footbridges and using steps to avoid problem areas. Keep an eye out for dippers and herons here. Do not cross the stepping stones when you reach them, but climb the steps, left and then turn right to regain the riverside route. You'll eventually walk a bund between the river and a millpond before reaching Gibson Mill **F**.

Cross the old toll bridge into the mill yard. This is the National Trust's flagship 'Green' project; an energy-neutral complex using hydroelectric power and recycling principles. There's an entry charge and it's easy to wile away an hour – there's also a **café** here, recalling the times when this was an unlikely entertainment centre in Edwardian days. Continue downstream, water on your right, to reach the graceful stone New Bridge at the woodland hamlet of Midgehole. Climb the steps to the lane but do not cross the bridge; instead turn left and walk to the tarred road; turn left and climb the hairpin access lane to the car park. ●

Cliviger Gorge

		GPS waypoints
Start	Holme Chapel	
Distance	6 miles (9.7km)	✎ SD 879 279
Height gain	1,750 feet (535m)	Ⓐ SD 873 277
		Ⓑ SD 871 271
Approximate time	4 hours	Ⓒ SD 886 260
Parking	Lay-by beside the A646, ½ mile	Ⓓ SD 898 262
	south east of Holme Chapel	Ⓔ SD 904 266
Route terrain	Two steep climbs and lots of rough,	Ⓕ SD 886 281
	boggy moorland walking	
Dog friendly	Several ladder-stiles near the end make this unsuitable for dogs	
Ordnance Survey maps	Landranger 103 (Blackburn & Burnley), Explorer OL21 (South Pennines)	

A remarkable gorge with precipitous crags, hanging woodlands and waterfalls that pepper the stark landscape; this walk visits both sides of the gorge, climbing to a medieval beacon site above the location of a silver mine. The going can be tough and steep; the walk is best not attempted in inclement weather.

✎ Facing the road from the lay-by, turn right along the pavement and walk the 200 yds to the driveway on the left for Pot Oven Farm – there's a bus stop here and a footpath fingerpost. Walk the drive past the house to the garage; here fork right on the walled track that drops to a footbridge across a beck. Cross this and climb the walled path into the fringe of Royd Wood. Use the hand-gate and turn right with the white waymark arrow; the path goes through another hand-gate and passes a bench. Keep ahead at a fork up the steep path, which snakes through an area of immature woodland (part of the new Burnley Forest), presently reaching a marker post near a wall and stone gatepost.

To your left is a large area of flat land at the foot of Thieveley Pike. Turn right on the path that rises past the knoll to reach a gate and hand-gate marked with a Burnley Way disc Ⓐ. The ruins nearby are at the site of a 17th century silver mine. During the last Ice Age, a vast meltwater lake here overflowed south, creating the dramatic Cliviger Gorge 13,000 years ago.

Use the hand-gate and join the faint field track, which rises near to the fence on your left. As this bends left around the top of the deep gash, keep ahead up to and straight across a fell road, a small cairn and Burnley Way marker confirming your route uphill on a thin path, eventually reaching the triangulation pillar at Thieveley Pike .

Turn left along the fence-line; climb the nearby stile and turn left on a track that gradually peels away from the fence, passing by a stone marking the ancient Limersgate trade route. Use the gate-side stile at the walled corner and go ahead with the wall on your right. In 200 yds this wall and accompanying track turn away right; at this juncture keep straight ahead, heading roughly for the left-hand pylon peeking above the horizon. Initially there's no discernible path, but one soon develops, a wide and often boggy way through typical Pennine upland country of pools, haggs and drifts of cotton grass. If in doubt, aim right of the distant landmark of Stoodley Pike's tower; a ½ mile walk will bring you to a waymarker post on the low, rounded top of Heald Moor .

Turn left on a clear path, which drops to a stile over a wall in a dip, shortly reaching a track. Turn left along this, enjoying the view down the sharp valley of the Calder over the mill village of Portsmouth. This track passes left of a renovated barn (bear right at the old stile and stay on the track) and winds all the way down to the main road in Portsmouth. Cross over, turn right and walk past **The Roebuck** pub to a lane on the left and a footpath fingerpost for Kebs Road .

SCALE 1:26316 or 2½ INCHES to 1 MILE 3.8CM to 1KM

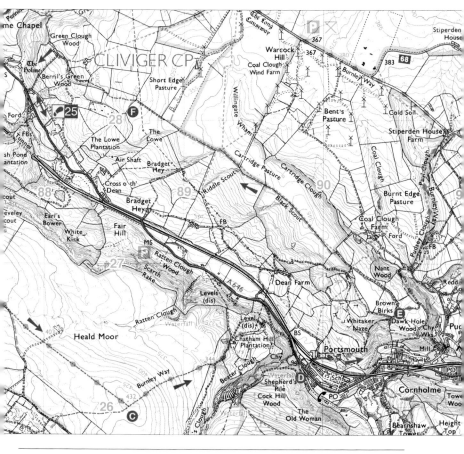

Calder Valley

Turn left here, Station Parade, use the railway crossing (take care) and join the rising lane beyond, allotments on your right. At the end use the stile and walk up the field path, keeping left at the fork (Burnley Way) up the steeper approach. Beyond a wall-gap, stay on the main path, which shortly threads around the head of a pretty wooded clough and passes piles of stones marking an old barn. At the fork, keep on the higher path to reach a corner of walls, fences and a stile **E**. Do not use the stile, but turn left and walk the rising path beside the wall on your right. A pleasant, springy grass path undulates to further ruins; here jig right through the gap in the low ridge and turn left alongside the fence. At a gate, turn left your side of it to a higher gate, use this one and stride ahead beside the wall/fence on your right.

This is an uncompromising moorland walk, with boggy flushes, tussocky reeds and marshy areas, with Coal Clough Wind Farm dominating the near horizon. Stay close to the wall, at one point using a corner gate to swap sides before re-crossing at a ladder-stile, near switch-gear, turning right here.

At the corner allow the wall to turn right **F**; you head slightly left at the waymarked post, putting a reedy beck on your immediate right. Climb another ladder-stile and, at the nearby post, pick a way through the marshy beck and turn left above it. The clough deepens as the path narrows to a track between it and a wall on the right, soon gaining a farm lane. Turn right and bend left to a stile beside an electronic gate; then walk to the farmhouse. On the left, immediately before the house, cross the lawn to the corner stile and drop down the left-edge of the haymeadow to a hand-gate into woods. The path drops steeply down the right edge of this plantation; at the foot use the gate and turn right past the barn to the main road. Turn left back to the lay-by. ●

Langfield Common, Stoodley Pike & Cragg Vale

		GPS waypoints
Start	Walsden Railway Station	⬛ SD 931 222
Finish	Mytholmroyd Railway Station – regular daily trains on the Halifax to Manchester Victoria line link these two stations, as do buses (Metroline Info: 0113 245 7676)	Ⓐ SD 939 217
		Ⓑ SD 938 226
		Ⓒ SD 973 242
		Ⓓ SD 991 241
Distance	10 miles (16km)	Ⓔ SE 000 232
Height gain	1,115 feet (340m)	Ⓕ SE 005 236
Approximate time	4½ hours	Ⓖ SE 007 251
Parking	Limited roadside parking nearby, plus a small village car park	
Route terrain	Largely good tracks and paths, may be muddy and a little marshy in a few places	
Ordnance Survey maps	Landranger 103 (Blackburn & Burnley), Explorer OL21 (South Pennines)	

This walk initially joins the well-worn route of a packhorse road that climbs steeply to Rake End. Leaving this at around 1,000ft, paths rise steadily onto Langfield Common, to reach the tower on Stoodley Pike, one of the South Pennines' best-known viewpoints. The descent into Mytholmroyd threads down along Cragg Vale, home to the renowned 'Coiners' in Georgian times.

⬛ From Walsden Railway Station cross the main road and join Alma Road, beside the chip shop. Turn right along the nearby towpath of the Rochdale Canal and walk this through to Bridge 35, near St Peter's Church. Cross the canal at the lock here and bear right along Birks Lane. This bends left past a derelict mill, passes beside a copse and then bends sharp right as Hollingworth Lane, rising through the woods and passing secluded houses to reach the gates to 'Towneley Trail' house Ⓐ. Turn left here, joining the Pennine Bridleway along Salter Gate Rake, shortly using a gate. This is the old packhorse route to the moors, a silver-grey thread across the grassy moor; it climbs steadily out of the valley to reach a junction in just over ½ mile, a location marked by a cairn and low waymarked post at Rake End Ⓑ.

Turn right on the rising path and walk this constantly uphill to reach the lake at Gaddings Dam, built in the 1830s to supply water to Lumbutts waterwheel tower in the valley below near Mankinholes. Along the way are memorable views off into the chasm of Summit Pass. Skirt to the left of the water; at the second corner, at a small beach, leave the lake and keep ahead

Stoodley Pike from Langfield Common

passes by a tall marker stone at Withens Gate before continuing to reach Stoodley Pike **C**.

This sturdy memorial commemorates Napoleon's abdication in 1814 and was completed after Wellington's final victory at Waterloo in 1815. There's a dark spiral staircase up to the viewing platform here, but you do not need to use this to appreciate the fabulous, 360-degree panorama from this, the most familiar and famous of the South Pennines' many viewpoints.

along the redundant stone dam. At the far end of this, slip slightly left to join the line of an old catchwater drain. It's a largely level path that presently parts company with the insubstantial drain at the edge of a clough. Allow the main path to turn sharp left into the gully; you should keep ahead on a lesser path which continues towards the head of the clough before curving left close to the steep Langfield Edge.

In the middle distance, the monument on Stoodley Pike takes the eye; it's simply a matter of ignoring any path that starts to descend left; remaining with the higher path which presently joins the route of the Pennine Way and

Head for the woods – a good path strikes from the tower to the conifer plantation to the east. A ladder-stile leads to a wide fire-break through the woods; at the cross-fire break turn left with the fingerpost for Cragg Road and walk to this walled moorland road. Turn right along this; 100 yds before the farmhouse turn right **D** on another walled track (signed for Stoodley Pike) and then look for the waymarked stile on the left at the end of the first field. Drop down the marshy right edge of this to reach a lane at the field-foot. Turn right momentarily; then go left on another walled track. This shortly bends left through the edge of a broadleaf

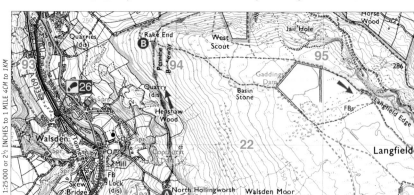

wood; remain on it to pass a remote farmhouse. At the junction fork right and remain on the winding lane all the way to the valley floor, keeping downhill at any junctions. Bear left at the ornate gatehouse to reach the river bridge **E**.

Cross the bridge and turn left at the foot of the churchyard here at Cragg Vale along a road marked as private. This winds through the fold of cottages and a small old mill; a gate leads into woodside paddocks with the Cragg Brook on your immediate left. This is the start of a superb walk down this tranquil valley. It was not always so; the Cragg Vale Coiners were a brotherhood of counterfeiters based in the Calder Valley and its, in the mid-

1700s, remote and inaccessible tributary valleys. Many, including the 'King' of the Coiners, David Hartley, were Cragg Vale residents. Their practice, of clipping shards of gold from legal tender coins, re-forging this into copies and using these as coin-of-the-realm, was so rife that they came close to debasing the whole currency. Excise men and troops eventually extinguished the practice in 1769 – justice was vengeful, with several coiners being hanged for the murder of an excise officer.

At the next bridge do not cross it, but walk ahead along the lane, passing by secluded houses. Just before reaching the main valley road, fork left – there's a yellow waymark painted on a stone – to pass directly in front of the house at

MAP CONTINUES ON PAGE 84 →

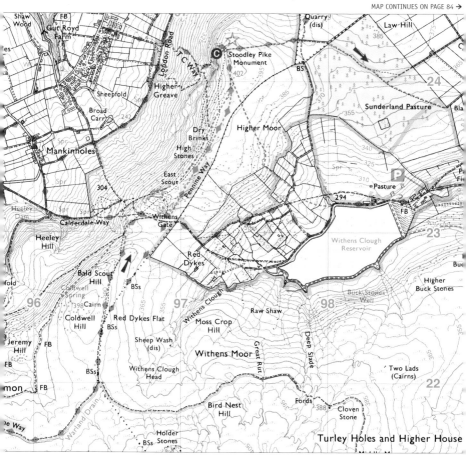

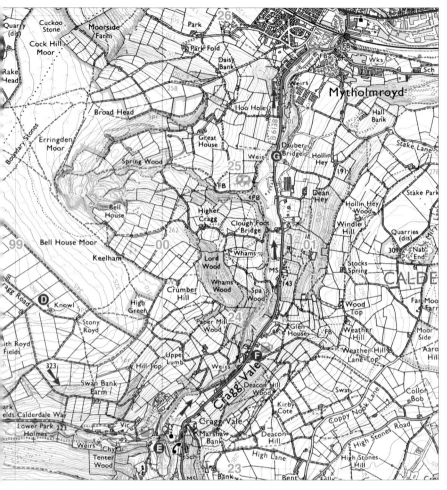

Castlegate Mill **F** and down a narrow concreted path. At the end turn left to cross the nearby bridge amid the tumbled ruins of an old mill and then turn right through the gate beside Papermill Cottage, joining a rising path through the woods, beside a wall on your left. *It's an occasionally thin and difficult-underfoot path, with precipitous drops to the right into the pretty gorge.* About 75 yds beyond the end of the wall, fork right at a waymarker post and drop down the path towards the beck. Use a wood-edge hand-gate and go ahead through paddocks to gain a tarred driveway. Descend this for 20 paces to find a

permissive path for Clough Foot Bridge; join this riverside route and continue downstream to reach the bridge. Do not cross it, but turn left for a few yards to find a fingerpost on the right, signed for Dauber Bridge.

The path skirts the top of pasture and shortly diverts left to cross a flat bridge over a side-beck before bending right to rejoin the route high above Cragg Brook. Upon reaching a concrete farm track, turn right and walk this through to the main road at Dauber Bridge **G**. Turn left and walk downhill to find the centre of Mytholmroyd and the railway station near the **Shoulder of Mutton Inn**.

Cononley, Lothersdale & Holme Beck Valley

		GPS waypoints
Start	Cononley	✐ SD 990 468
Distance	8 miles (13km)	Ⓐ SD 966 473
Height gain	1,505 feet (460m)	Ⓑ SD 958 459
Approximate time	4½ hours	Ⓒ SD 969 444
Parking	Roadside parking near the post office	Ⓓ SD 980 443
		Ⓔ SD 984 455
Route terrain	Short, steep section near the start, but mostly easy going on lanes, tracks and field paths	
Dog friendly	Lots of stiles make this unsuitable for dogs	
Ordnance Survey maps	Landranger 103 (Blackburn & Burnley), Explorer OL21 (South Pennines)	

A softer, gentler side of the South Pennines is visited on this walk between pretty villages tucked away in tributary valleys of the River Aire, just a stone's throw away from Skipton, where the Yorkshire Dales assume the mantle of the Pennines. From the former lead-mining centre of Cononley, lanes and tracks ripple over low ridges to secluded Lothersdale; its mill chimney, pub and pond are all familiar landmarks to walkers on the Pennine Way. Beck-side paths and lanes meandering between haymeadows thread back past an old lead mine to the start.

✐ Walk up Cononley's main street, with the Pismire Beck on your left and the **New Inn** on your right. At the fork above the Village Institute, capped by its clock tower, keep left for Lothersdale and walk this lane, steep in places, to a T-junction. Along the way, old cottages huddle deep in this winding clough beneath hillsides disturbed by lead-miners, occasional spoil tips and rakes patterning the landscape. At the T-junction, cross to use the right-hand field gate, joining a field-side track that continues to rise gently towards the distant ridge line. Off to your left is the most substantial remnant of the lead-mining industry, the engine-house and chimney of the steam-powered Cornish beam engine that once powered the pumps and drove the lifting machinery at Cononley Mine. Gates take the faint track up to a remote farmhouse at Street Head; pass to the right in front of this, joining the driveway to reach a hilltop lane Ⓐ.

Turn left along this elevated road, harvesting the fine views to all points of the compass, a heady mix of moorland edge reedy pastures, haymeadows, pocket woods and cloughs. At a fork in 400 yds, take the rougher lane to the right, signed as a 'Restricted Byway'.

This, Tow Top Lane, shortly crests to reveal the deep, secluded Lothersdale, secreted in the folded hills. The lane drops towards the village, dominated by its slender old mill chimney. At the point the lane bends sharply right, keep ahead on the walled green track; this issues into a steep, marshy field pock-marked by old workings, head for the diagonally opposite lower corner where a gate leads into a sunken track down to the village road. Turn right and walk to the **Hare & Hounds Inn** 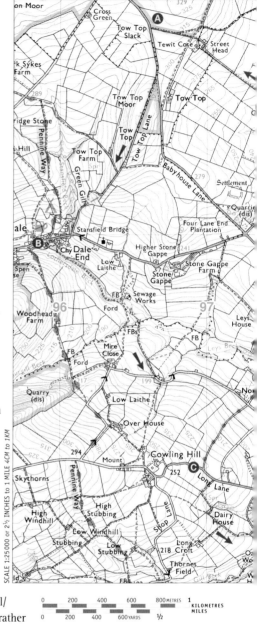 at the heart of this pretty little settlement, huddled around the old spinning mill, which was built in 1792 at a cost of £1,500. The millpond is slightly higher up the valley; the mill race surges below the pub's car park.

With your back to the pub, slip left down the lane leading to and through the mill yard. Upon reaching Peel Terrace, turn right in front of Mill Cottage and walk to the gate at the foot of the chimney. A lovely beck-side stroll ensues, swiftly leaving the village behind. Pass by the sewage works on the far bank and remain beside the beck to your left for a further 150 yds or so. As the reedy field narrows, look carefully ahead right for a footbridge and stile beneath an electricity pole. Use the stile and turn uphill with a wall/fence on your right, climbing this rather boggy field to reach a gap-stile beside a gate in the top-right corner. A path threads up this wooded corridor to gain a narrow lane beside a house.

Turn left and walk this lane for nearly ½ mile. Across the valley is an imposing Georgian mansion, Stone Gappe House. At one time a youth hostel, it features as Gateshead Hall in Charlotte Brontë's *Jane Eyre;* Brontë spent a short period as governess to the Sidgwick family children here. At the far end of a long walled garden on your left, turn right up a tree-shaded old track, which rises easily to reach another lane 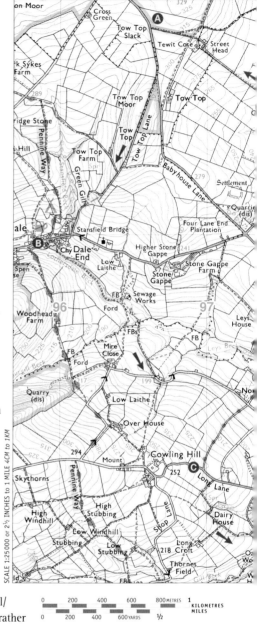. Ahead

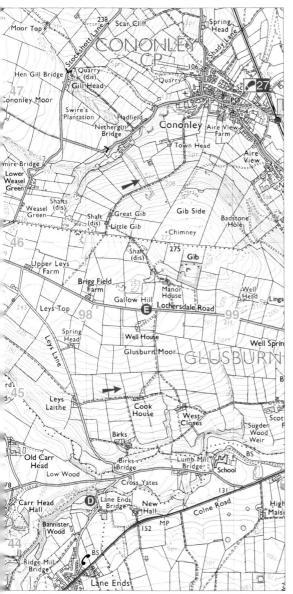

70 yds short of houses. On the left here is a gateway and nearby stable, walk past this to the lane and turn right. Where the tarred lane bends right, keep ahead on the green track; beyond a gate drop down the track to reach a beck-side path and turn left, downstream beside Holme Beck. The path runs above the beck, passing an unusual old open gateway over a side stream. Shortly after this, keep your eyes peeled for an indistinct fork in the path (beneath two very tall ash trees) where you should go right, down awkward stone steps to find and cross a long, narrow wooden footbridge to gain a lane **D**.

Turn left along this, re-cross the beck and walk steeply up to the junction. Look slightly left for a narrow squeeze-stile, drop down the steps here and fall to another squeeze-stile onto a lower lane. Turn left, cross Birks Bridge and rise with the lane to reach a point immediately before Leys Laithe Farm on your left. On the right, a footpath fingerpost indicates the onward route over a stone stile and along the foot of several sloping pastures, presently passing behind the isolated cottage at Cook House. Turn left up the rough field track here and trace this, via several gates, up to Lothersdale Road **E**.

of you is the line of Earl Crag, with Cowling village strung out across its lower flank.

Turn left along the lane; in 100 yds take the driveway to the right and walk round to the house. Take the entry to the right immediately before the building, go through a field gate on the left and stick to the left side of the fields, falling gradually to reach a point

Turn right; in 150 yds go left up the drive to Manor House Farm. Pass immediately right of the building and bend left into the constricted back yard. Leave via the gate and walk ahead across the farmyard, shortly starting to bend gradually right up a dirt road through a huge selection of redundant tractors. Pass through the gateway at an offset wall corner and favour the lower, level field track ahead. To your left are the remains of part of the mining complex here at Gib Hill. Use the ladder-stile at the top corner of the field and head for the left one of two houses at the foot of the next meadow. Behind this is the restored engine house of Cononley Lead Mine. You'll find a stone step-stile virtually in front of the farmhouse; turn right on the tarred track for 20 paces before using another stile beside a gate. Walk behind the second house; over a gate-side stone stile and then ahead on a field road which runs alongside a wall on your left. Stick with this, which shortly passes below a spoil tip and across the line of a rake, which strikes down the hillside to the cottages in the valley bottom.

The track eventually becomes a walled way, dropping to merge with a tarred driveway. Keep downhill on this, walking through to reach the top of Cononley's main street. Turn right to return to the village centre. ●

Lothersdale from Top Tow Lane; the Hare and Hounds beckons

Wycoller & Boulsworth Hill

		GPS waypoints
Start	Ball Grove Picnic Site, Colne	🖊 SD 908 401
Distance	9¼ miles (15km)	Ⓐ SD 922 405
Height gain	1,735 feet (530m)	Ⓑ SD 932 392
Approximate time	5 hours	Ⓒ SD 940 379
Parking	Picnic Site signed from the A6068 at the eastern fringe of Colne, off Cotton Tree Lane	Ⓓ SD 933 372
		Ⓔ SD 929 356
		Ⓕ SD 927 369
Route terrain	Field paths, village lanes, farm tracks and open moorland. One steep climb and several steady climbs	Ⓖ SD 918 373
		Ⓗ SD 912 392
Dog friendly	There are several difficult stiles and ladder-stiles; Access Land restrictions apply	
Ordnance Survey maps	Landranger 103 (Blackburn & Burnley), Explorer OL21 (South Pennines)	

This challenging walk explores the wild countryside of the Forest of Trawden, where high grouse moors ripple to the highest point in the South Pennines. Visiting the charming hamlet of Wycoller, with its Brontë connections, tracks and paths rise increasingly steeply across rough country to Boulsworth Hill and its summit of Lad Law 1,696ft (517m) high. Cracking views and solitude tempt you to linger before dropping into the valley of Trawden Beck with its hidden waterfalls and the little mill town of Trawden.

🖊 Join the path between the river and playground, walking upstream through a nature reserve. Beyond the top pond, cross the footbridge into an enclosed, stepped path which crosses more footbridges to reach a lane near cottages Ⓐ. Cross straight over onto a field path beside the beck; the horizon is dominated by the long ridge of Boulsworth Hill. The Pendle Way is well waymarked through to a lane at Wycoller; turn left into the hamlet. The slim, askew packhorse bridge and nearby clapper bridge are testament to a long history; the ruined Wycoller Hall is said to have been the inspiration for

Ferndean Manor in Charlotte Brontë's *Jane Eyre*.

Cross the bridge Ⓑ and turn right on the rough lane past the ruins, continuing upstream past the steeply angled Clam Bridge, another ancient clapper bridge. At a sharp-left band, use the hand-gate on your right, joining a field path up Turnhole Clough. At the nearby waymarked post keep ahead on the path above the beck, cross a footbridge and remain beside a fence above the water. Slip through another hand-gate but do not cross the footbridge here; rather, turn right up the dell. The path breaks free of the woods;

beyond another hand-gate it rises to a final gate onto a bridleway above a substantial wooden bridge 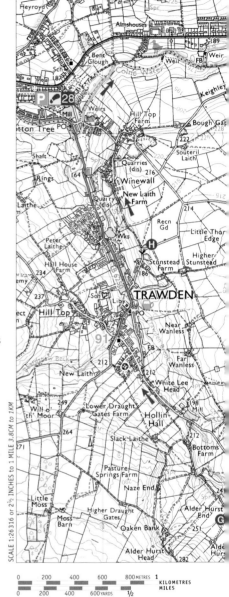 C.

Bear right on the developing rough track to skirt the break of slope high above Saucer Hill Clough. The steep, scored, reedy slopes of Boulsworth Hill are one candidate for the *Wuthering Heights* of Emily Brontë's novel. The track bends right beside a substantial moorland-edge estate wall. In contrast to the dour slopes, the view right is a superb prospect across central Lancashire to Pendle Hill and the Dales beyond. In $^1\!/_2$ mile a tarred lane joins from the right D.

Do not join the tarred lane, but turn left up the field road. This grassy, gravelled track winds up rough pastures beside Saucer Hill Beck, through one field-gate to reach a second. Climb the wood-rail stile and continue on the faint, grassy track beyond up the steep flank of Boulsworth Hill to reach the ridge-crest near the Little Saucer Stones. Turn right and walk past eroded crowns of gritstone to reach the trig pillar marking Lad Law E, the highest point in the South Pennines. On clear days, views from here are astonishing.

The way down is along the well-walked path that heads just west of the distant bulk of Pendle Hill; yellow-topped posts confirm the route past further stone outcrops and eventually beside a wall (right) to reach a rough lane. Turn right and walk past the farmhouse to reach a barn, where the lane becomes tarred. Keep ahead another 50 paces to use a hand-gate on the left, just past a field gate F. Go ahead with the wall on your left, climb a ladder-stile and start down the shallow cleft of the clough ahead, dropping to a flat concrete bridge. Turn left immediately before this, putting the little clough on your right. Shortly, the

sound of a waterfall reveals this hidden gem, a popular picnic place in Edwardian times; there was even a café here. Use a stile and remain with the falling path above the beck, cross a footbridge, then bear right across the banana-bridge over side streams. Climb a stile and walk left up the grassy bank to a lane left of houses G.

Turn right and stay with it past cottages and farms to reach the road at

SCALE 1:26316 or 2½ INCHES to 1 MILE 3.8CM to 1KM

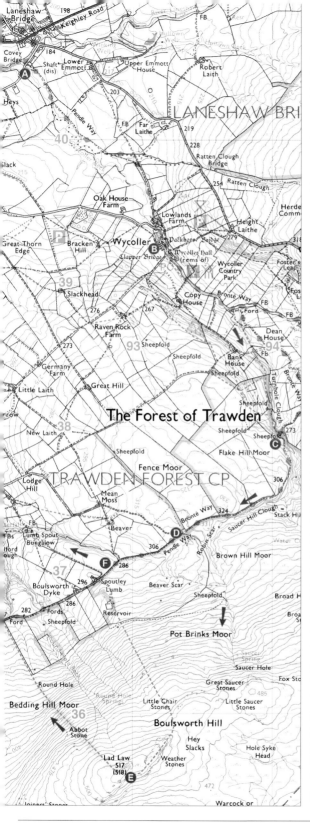

the top of Trawden; turn left along this past the converted mill and picturesque old terraced cottages to reach a bus-turning circle on the right. Bear right here along the old tramway (closed 1928), a cobbled ginnel that falls to a junction beside the **Trawden Arms** pub. Turn right; in another 150 yds turn right at the War Memorial on a road signed for Wycoller, rising steeply to a sharp-right bend **H**.

Fork left on the waymarked path, walk past pigeon-lofts and trace the wide, grassy track across the hillside; to your left are grand views across the archetypical little mill town of Trawden. On reaching housing at the hamlet of Winewall bend gradually right; the track soon becomes tarred, here keep gradually uphill to pass by a grave-yard. At the sharp bend, turn downhill to return to the car park. ●

Further Information

Safety on the Hills

The hills, mountains and moorlands of Britain, though of modest height compared with those in many other countries, need to be treated with respect. Friendly and inviting in good weather, they can quickly be transformed into wet, misty, windswept and potentially dangerous areas of wilderness in bad weather. Even on an outwardly fine and settled summer day, conditions can rapidly deteriorate at high altitudes and, in winter, even more so.

Therefore it is advisable to always take both warm and waterproof clothing, sufficient nourishing food, a hot drink, first-aid kit, torch and whistle. Wear suitable footwear, such as strong walking boots or shoes that give a good grip over rocky terrain and on slippery slopes. Try to obtain a local weather forecast and bear it in mind before you start. Do not be afraid to abandon your proposed route and return to your starting point in the event of a sudden and unexpected deterioration in the weather. Do not go alone and allow enough time to finish the walk well before nightfall.

Most of the walks described in this book do not venture into remote wilderness areas and will be safe to do, given due care and respect, at any time of year in all but the most unreasonable weather. Indeed, a crisp, fine winter day often provides perfect walking conditions, with firm ground underfoot and a clarity that is not possible to achieve in the other seasons of the year. A few walks, however, are suitable only for reasonably fit and experienced hill walkers able to use a compass and should definitely not be tackled by anyone else during the winter months or in bad weather, especially high winds and mist. These are indicated in the general description that precedes each of the walks.

Walkers and the Law

The Countryside and Rights of Way Act

(*CRoW Act 2000*) extends the rights of access previously enjoyed by walkers in England and Wales. Implementation of these rights began on 19 September 2004. The Act amends existing legislation and for the first time provides access on foot to certain types of land – defined as mountain, moor, heath, down and registered common land.

Where You Can Go
Rights of Way
Prior to the introduction of the CRoW Act, walkers could only legally access the countryside along public rights of way. These are either 'footpaths' (for walkers only) or 'bridleways' (for walkers, riders on horseback and pedal cyclists). A third category called 'Byways open to all traffic' (BOATs), is used by motorised vehicles as well as those using non-mechanised transport. Mainly they are green lanes, farm and estate roads, although occasionally they will be found crossing mountainous area.

Rights of way are marked on Ordnance Survey maps. Look for the green broken lines on the Explorer maps, or the red dashed lines on Landranger maps.

The term 'right of way' means exactly what it says. It gives a right of passage over what, for the most part, is private land. Under pre-CRoW legislation walkers were required to keep to the line of the right of way and not stray onto land on either side. If you did inadvertently wander off the right of way, either because of faulty map reading or because the route was not clearly indicated on the ground, you were technically trespassing.

Local authorities have a legal obligation to ensure that rights of way are kept clear and free of obstruction, and are signposted where they leave metalled roads. The duty of local authorities to install signposts extends to the placing of signs along a path or way, but only where the authority considers it necessary to have a signpost or

Countryside Access Charter

Your rights of way are:

- public footpaths – on foot only. Sometimes waymarked in yellow
- bridle-ways – on foot, horseback and pedal cycle. Sometimes waymarked in blue
- byways (usually old roads), most 'roads used as public paths' and, of course, public roads – all traffic has the right of way

Use maps, signs and waymarks to check rights of way. Ordnance Survey Explorer and Landranger maps show most public rights of way

On rights of way you can:

- take a pram, pushchair or wheelchair if practicable
- take a dog (on a lead or under close control)
- take a short route round an illegal obstruction or remove it sufficiently to get past

You have a right to go for recreation to:

- public parks and open spaces – on foot
- most commons near older towns and cities – on foot and sometimes on horseback
- private land where the owner has a formal agreement with the local authority

In addition you can use the following by local or established custom or consent, but ask for advice if you are unsure:

- many areas of open country, such as moorland, fell and coastal areas, especially those in the care of the National Trust, and some commons
- some woods and forests, especially those owned by the Forestry Commission
- country parks and picnic sites
- most beaches
- canal towpaths
- some private paths and tracks Consent sometimes extends to horse-riding and cycling

For your information:

- county councils and London boroughs maintain and record rights of way, and register commons
- obstructions, dangerous animals, harassment and misleading signs on rights of way are illegal and you should report them to the county council
- paths across fields can be ploughed, but must normally be reinstated within two weeks
- landowners can require you to leave land to which you have no right of access
- motor vehicles are normally permitted only on roads, byways and some 'roads used as public paths'

waymark to assist persons unfamiliar with the locality.

The New Access Rights
Access Land

As well as being able to walk on existing rights of way, under the new legislation you now have access to large areas of open land. You can of course continue to use rights of way footpaths to cross this land, but the main difference is that you can now lawfully leave the path and wander at will, but only in areas designated as access land.

Where to Walk

Areas now covered by the new access rights – Access Land – are shown on Ordnance Survey Explorer maps bearing the access land symbol on the front cover.

'Access Land' is shown on Ordnance Survey maps by a light yellow tint surrounded by a pale orange border. New orange coloured 'i' symbols on the maps will show the location of permanent access information boards installed by the access authorities.

Restrictions

The right to walk on access land may lawfully be restricted by landowners. Landowners can, for any reason, restrict access for up to 28 days in any year. They cannot however close the land:

- on bank holidays;
- for more than four Saturdays and

Sundays in a year;
- on any Saturday from 1 June to 11 August; or
- on any Sunday from 1 June to the end of September.

They have to provide local authorities with five working days' notice before the date of closure unless the land involved is an area of less than five hectares or the closure is for less than four hours. In these cases land-owners only need to provide two hours' notice.

Whatever restrictions are put into place on access land they have no effect on existing rights of way, and you can continue to walk on them.

Dogs

Dogs can be taken on access land, but must be kept on leads of two metres or less between 1 March and 31 July, and at all times where they are near livestock. In addition landowners may impose a ban on all dogs from fields where lambing takes place for up to six weeks in any year. Dogs may be banned from moorland used for grouse shooting and breeding for up to five years.

In the main, walkers following the routes in this book will continue to follow existing rights of way, but a knowledge and understanding of the law as it affects walkers, plus the ability to distinguish access land marked on the maps, will enable anyone who wishes to depart from paths that cross access land either to take a shortcut, to enjoy a view or to explore.

General Obstructions

Obstructions can sometimes cause a problem on a walk and the most common of these is where the path across a field has been ploughed over. It is legal for a farmer to plough up a path provided that it is restored within two weeks. This does not always happen and you are faced with the dilemma of following the line of the path, even if this means treading on crops, or walking round the edge of the field. Although the later course of action seems

the most sensible, it does mean that you would be trespassing.

Other obstructions can vary from overhanging vegetation to wire fences across the path, locked gates or even a cattle feeder on the path.

Use common sense. If you can get round the obstruction without causing damage, do so. Otherwise only remove as much of the obstruction as is necessary to secure passage.

If the right of way is blocked and cannot be followed, there is a long-standing view that in such circumstances there is a right to deviate, but this cannot wholly be relied on. Although it is accepted in law that highways (and that includes rights of way) are for the public service, and if the usual track is impassable, it is for the general good that people should be entitled to pass into another line. However, this should not be taken as indicating a right to deviate whenever a way becomes impassable. If in doubt, retreat.

Report obstructions to the local authority and/or The Ramblers.

 ## Useful Organisations

Campaign to Protect Rural England
128 Southwark Street,
London SE1 0SW
Tel. 020 7981 2800
www.cpre.org.uk

Long Distance Walker's Association
www.ldwa.org.uk

National Trust
Membership and general enquiries
PO Box 39, Warrington WA5 7WD
Tel. 0844 800 1895
www.nationaltrust.org.uk
Lancashire Regional Office
Stamford Estates, 18 High Street,
Altrincham, Cheshire WA14 1PH
Tel. 0161 928 0075
Yorkshire Regional Office
Goddards, 27 Tadcaster Road,
Dringhouses, York YO24 1GG
Tel. 01904 702 021

Natural England
Yorkshire
Government Buildings,
Otley Road, Lawnswood,
Leeds LS16 5QT
Tel. 0113 230 3750
www.naturalengland.org.uk
Lancashire
The Annex, Barton Hall,
Garstang Road, Barton,
Preston PR3 5HE
Tel. 01772 865 224

Ordnance Survey
Romsey Road, Maybush,
Southampton SO16 4GU
Tel. 08456 05 05 05 (lo-call)
www.ordnancesurvey.co.uk

Peak & Northern Footpaths Society
Taylor House, 23 Turncroft Lane,
Offerton, Stockport SK1 4AB
Tel. 0161 480 3565
www.peakandnorthern.org.uk

The Ramblers
2nd Floor, Camelford House, 87-90 Albert
Embankment, London SE1 7TW
Tel. 0207 339 8500
www.ramblers.org.uk

Youth Hostels Association
Trevelyan House, Dimple Road, Matlock,
Derbyshire DE4 3YH
Tel. 01629 592 600
www.yha.org.uk

Rights of way
Any blockages, collapses or maintenance
problems encountered on the walks in this
book should be notified to the Public Rights
of Way team at the appropriate local
authority:

Bradford Tel. 01274 432666
Calderdale Tel. 01422 357 257
Kirklees Tel. 01484 221 000
Oldham Tel. 0161 620 8202
Pendle Tel. 01282 661 059
Rochdale Tel. 01706 647474
Other Lancashire areas Tel. 01772 534 709

Tourist information centres:
Burnley: Tel. 01282 455 485
Halifax: Tel. 01422 368 725
Haworth: Tel. 01535 642 329
Hebden Bridge: Tel. 01422 843 831
Holmfirth: Tel. 01484 222 444
Huddersfield: Tel. 01484 223 200
Ilkley: Tel. 01943 602 319
Littleborough: Tel. 01706 378 481
Oldham: Tel. 0161 627 1024
Rawtenstall: Tel. 01706 244 678
Rochdale: Tel. 01706 864 928
Saddleworth: Tel. 01457 870 336
Skipton: Tel. 01756 792 809
Todmorden: Tel. 01706 818 181

 Ordnance Survey maps of the South & West Pennine areas

The Pennines are covered by Ordnance
Survey 1:50 000 scale (1 ¼ inches to 1 mile
or 2cm to 1km) Landranger sheets 103, 104,
109 and 110. These all-purpose maps are
packed with information to help you
explore the area. Viewpoints, picnic sites,
places of interest, caravan and camping
sites are shown, as well as public rights of
way information such as footpaths and
bridleways.

To examine the Pennines in more detail,
and especially if you are planning walks,
Ordnance Survey Explorer maps at
1:25 000 (2 ½ inches to 1 mile or 4cm to
1km) scale are ideal.

277 (Manchester & Salford)
288 (Bradford & Huddersfield)
297 (Lower Wharfedale & Washburn Valley)
OL1 The Peak District (Dark Peak area)
OL21 South Pennines

To get to the South Pennines, use the
Ordnance Survey OS Travel Map-Route
Great Britain at 1:625 000 scale (1 inch to
10 miles or 4cm to 25km) or Road Map 4
(Northern England) at 1: 250 000 scale (1
inch to 4 miles or 1cm to 2.5km).
Ordnance Survey maps and guides are
available from most booksellers, stationers
and newsagents.